Copyright © 2012 Jo Franks

Table of Contents

Table of Contents iii
Preface v

Chapter 1

A–M 1
    Adriatic Ravioli 1
    Beurre Blanc for Lamb Spirals 2
    Broccoli Pesto Cheese Ravioli 3
    Carrots, Goat Cheese, Thyme And Sun-Dried Tomatoes 4
    Celery Root Ravioli With Celery/Mushroom Filling 4
    Chicken Catchatory-Ravioli Stew 5
    Chicken Ravioli 7
    Chocolate-Filled Ravioli Cookie 8
    Duck Confit And Mashed Potato Ravioli W White Truffle Sauce 9
    Easy Chicken Ravioli 10
    Eggplant-Filled Ravioli With Tomato Cream Sauce 11
    Filo Ravioli With Apples And Pears 13
    Fried Ravioli 15
    Hazelnut Squash Ravioli Filling 15
    Herbal Ravioli On Poached Tomatoes And Basil 16
    Inside Out Ravioli 17
    Inside Out Ravioli – 1 18
    Inside Out Ravioli – 2 19
    Lamb Spirals with Goat Cheese Ravioli 20
    Lemony Chicken & Anchovy Ravioli 21
    Mock Ravioli 22

Chapter 2

N–Z 24
    Pansotti Triangles With Artichokes Like Genoa's 24
    Perfect Saffron Pasta 25
    Poppy Seed Ravioli Cookies 27

Potato Ravioli With Butter Sage 28
Potstickers – 1 29
Pumpkin Ravioli 32
Pumpkin Ravioli In Chicken Broth 33
Purim Ravioli 34
Ramp Ravioli With One-Hour Calamari 35
Ravioli 36
Ravioli Appetizers 37
Ravioli Casserole 38
Ravioli di Zucchine e Gamberi 38
Ravioli Genovese 40
Ravioli Soup 41
Ravioli Vegetable 'Lasagna' 41
Ravioli With Herb-Tomato Sauce 43
Ravioli With Broccoli Sauce 44
Ravioli With Ricotta Filling 45
Rosemary Chicken Breasts, Brown Butter And Balsamic Ravioli 46
Southwestern Won Ton Ravioli 47
Spicy Vegetable Vinaigrette 49
St. Louis Toasted Ravioli 49
Summer Vegetable Ravioli With Spicy Vinaigrette 50
Sweet Pepper Ravioli (Adapted From William-Sonoma Pasta) 52
Swordfish Ravioli With Olive Pesto 53
Toasted Ravioli 54
Turkey Cutlets With Fried Ravioli 54
Vegetable Filled Ravioli 56
White Bean Ravioli With Balsamic Vinegar Brown Butter 57
White Chocolate Ravioli 58
White Meat Ravioli 60
Wild Mushroom Ravioli With Eggplant And Goat Cheese 61
Wonton Skin Raviolis 62

Index **64**

Preface

Notice of Rights

All rights reserved. No part of this book may be reproduced or transmitted in any form by any means, electronic, mechanical, photocopying, recording, or otherwise, without the prior written permission of the publisher.

Notice of Liability

The information in this book is distributed on an "As Is" basis without warranty. While every precaution has been taken in the preparation of the book, neither the author nor the publisher shall have any liability to any person or entity with respect to any loss or damage caused or alleged to be caused directly or indirectly by the instructions contained in this book or by the products described in it.

Trademarks

Many of the designations used by manufacturers and sellers to distinguish their products are claimed as trademarks. Where those designations appear in this book, and the publisher was aware of a trademark claim, the designations appear as requested by the owner of the trademark. All other product names and services identified throughout this book are used in editorial fashion only and for the benefit of such companies with no intention of infringement of the trademark. No such use, or the use of any trade name, is intended to convey endorsement or other affiliation with this book.

Jo Franks

Chapter 1
A–M

ADRIATIC RAVIOLI

4 servings
Source: Ravioli Greats

- 1 lb. **asparagus, fresh**
- 1 lb. **cheese ravioli, small, frozen**
- 5 tablespoons **butter, or margarine**
- 1 large **red bell pepper,** seeded and cut into
- 1 thin, 2-inch-long strips (1 cup)
- ½ lb. **mushrooms, thinly sliced** (about 2 cups)
- 4 large **garlic cloves,** peeled and minced
- 3 tablespoons **unbleached white flour**
- 2 ½ cups **milk**
- ¼ teaspoon **salt**
- 1 teaspoon **paprika, plus** additional for garnish
- 1 tablespoon **dijon mustard**
- ¼ cup **fresh basil, chopped**
- ½ cup **romano cheese, (2 ounces), finely** grated pepper finely grated parmesan cheese

Put a large pot of water on to boil. Snap off and discard the tough asparagus ends, and cut the stalks into 1-inch pieces. You will have about 3 cups of asparagus. Steam until barely tender, 6 to 8 minutes, and set aside.

Begin cooking the ravioli, stirring occasionally.

Melt 1 tablespoon of the butter in a skillet over medium heat. Saute the red pepper, mushrooms, and garlic until tender, 3 to 4 minutes. Remove the pan from the heat.

Melt the remaining 4 tablespoons butter in a large, heavy saucepan over medium heat. Whisk in the flour, and let it cook for a minute or two. Slowly pour in the milk, whisking constantly until thickened, about 3 to 5 minutes.

Add the salt, paprika, mustard, basil, Romano cheese, and pepper to taste stirring until the cheese is melted. Reduce the heat to very low, and stir in the sauted vegetables.

When the ravioli is tender and begins to float , after about 10 to 12 minutes, drain it well, and transfer it to a large serving bowl.

Pour on the sauce, and toss gently. Garnish with paprika, and serve with Parmesan on the side.

Tender ravioli, asparagus, and mushrooms tossed with a Dijon and basil cheese sauce make for this elegant entree, named for Italy's beautiful Adriatic coast.

BEURRE BLANC FOR LAMB SPIRALS

4 servings
Source: Ravioli Greats

2 shallots, chopped

1 tablespoon **cream**

¼ lb. **butter**

1 cup **white wine**

1 pinch **salt**, to taste

1 pinch **white pepper**, to taste

1 pinch **cayenne pepper**, to taste

Sweat shallots in butter, add white wine, a pinch each of salt, white pepper, and cayenne pepper. Reduce.

Add cream. Reduce. Whisk in butter over medium heat. Strain and keep warm.

BROCCOLI PESTO CHEESE RAVIOLI

1 servings
Source: Ravioli Greats

- **craig gardiner, (knht09a)**
- **1 head broccoli florets**
- 3 tablespoons **olive oil**
- 2 tablespoons **parmesan cheese, grated**
- 1 ½ teaspoons **lemon juice**
- ½ teaspoon **garlic, minced**
- ¼ teaspoon **salt**
- 2 tablespoons **walnuts pcs**
- ½ lb. **ravioli, cooked**
- 1 tablespoon **olive oil**
- 2 tablespoons **fresh basil, chopped for garnish**
- **parmesan cheese, grated**

Select the nicer half of the florets and reserve. Blanch the remainder in boiling water, refresh in cold water and then drain and dry them. Combine the blanched broccoli in the food processor with olive oil, cheese, lemon juice, garlic, and salt. Blend until smooth, then add walnuts and pulse until nuts are chopped.

Remove from bowl and set aside. Add the reserved broccoli florets to the pot a minute before ravioli are done. Drain ravioli and broccoli in a colander. Return warm pot to low heat and add olive oil.

Return ravioli and broccoli to pan and toss with sauce mixture and serve immediately in hot deep plates, garnished with fresh basil if desired. Pass additional grated Parmesan cheese.

CARROTS, GOAT CHEESE, THYME AND SUN-DRIED TOMATOES

4 servings
Source: Ravioli Greats

2 **large carrots, scrubbed**

8 **dried tomatoes, rehydrated, chopped**

fresh thyme, to taste

14 ounces **hot cooked pasta, drained**

1 tablespoon **olive oil**

8 ounces **goat cheese, grated**

OR **fresh parmesan**

salt and pepper

Heat a sauce pan with water to cook the carrots. Grate the carrots into long shreds, then cook for 1 minute in the pan of water. Drain and return to the pan; add the sun-dried tomatoes and some fresh thyme to taste.

Place hot pasta in a warmed serving bowl. Toss with olive oil, carrot mixture and cheese, salt and pepper to taste. Toss gently and serve on warm plates.

Notes: Use any flat pasta like farfalle, short broad egg noodle, or ravioli. Add a little citrus peel to the water used to rehydrate the tomatoes.

CELERY ROOT RAVIOLI WITH CELERY/MUSHROOM FILLING

4 servings
Source: Ravioli Greats

½ cup **diced carrot**

½ cup **diced celery**

½ cup **diced spanish onion**

6 teaspoons **olive oil**

2 **large celery roots, peeled**

3 **large portobello mushrooms**

salt and pepper

1 clove **garlic**

1 sprig **rosemary**

1 stalk **celery, diced**

Ravioli Greats

1 tablespoon **diced shallots**	2 cups **flat-leaf parsley leaves**
2 tablespoons **chopped fresh herbs, (e.g. parsley, chives)**	1 recipe red wine reduction, recipe follows

In a medium saucepan, caramelize the carrots, celery, and onion in 2 teaspoons of the olive oil. Add the celery root, cover three-quarters of the way with water, and cover the pan. Slowly braise for 45 to 60 minutes, or until tender. Remove the celery root from the braising liquid and cool completely. Reserve the braising liquid.

Trim the celery root to square off- and slice paper thin. Clean the Portobello mushrooms by removing the stems and the dark brown underside. Cut into quarters, season with salt and pepper, and drizzle with 2 teaspoons of the olive oil. Place in an ovenproof pan with the garlic and rosemary and cover with aluminum foil.

Bake at 350°F for 30 to 40 minutes, or until tender. In a medium sauté pan, saute the diced celery and shallot in 1 teaspoon of the olive oil. Dice the roasted mushrooms and toss with the celery mixture and herbs. In a saute pan, wilt the Italian parsley in 1 teaspoon of the olive oil and 1 tablespoon of the braising liquid. Place the celery root slices on a sheet pan with a dash of the braising liquid, season with salt and pepper, and bake at 350°F for 3 to 4 minutes to reheat.

Lay 1 slice of the celery root on a plate and top with the mushroom and celery mixture. Place a piece of the parsley on top and cover with another piece of the celery root. Press the edges of the celery root together and place small pinches of braised Italian parsley at each corner. Drizzle with Red Wine Reduction around the edges of each plate.

CHICKEN CATCHATORY-RAVIOLI STEW

4 servings
Source: Ravioli Greats

- 3 cloves **garlic**
- 2 tablespoons **extra-virgin olive oil**
- 2 sprigs **fresh rosemary leaves**
- 2 sprigs **fresh thyme leaves**
- 1 cup **pre-sliced fresh mushrooms**
- **Salt, to taste**
- **Freshly-ground black pepper, to taste**
- 1 can **stewed tomatoes with peppers, onions and celery - (15 oz)**
- 2 **roasted red peppers, drained**
- 1 cup **tomato sauce**
- 1 package **chopped frozen spinach, thawed, drained**
- 6 cups **chicken broth**
- 1 package **chicken breast tenders - (3/4 to 1 lb)**
- 1 lb. **fresh ravioli, any flavor**
- 1 cup **grated Parmigiano-Reggiano or Romano, to pass at table**
- **Crusty Italian bread or rolls, to pass at table**

Heat a big soup pot over medium-high heat.

Whack the garlic with a fist or the palm of your hand. Separate the skins from the smashed garlic and throw just the skins away into the garbage bowl. Whack the 3 cloves of garlic with the bottom of a small saucepan. Add extra-virgin olive oil, 2 turns of the pan, to the soup pot. Throw in the garlic and 2 stems each of the rosemary and fresh thyme herbs. The leaves will fall off the stems and give a delicious and really cool flavor to your special stew. Add the mushrooms, too and help stir as the mushrooms cook 3 to 5 minutes. Season the mushrooms up with a little salt and pepper as they're cooking.

Next, open the can of tomatoes and pour into the soup pot. Use a sharp, small knife to chop the red roasted bell peppers into bite-size pieces. Add the chopped up roasted red peppers to the tomatoes and stir. Squeeze as much liquid as possible out of the spinach. Add spinach, tomato sauce and chicken broth to the pot. Stir until the spinach is all broken up in the broth. Cover the soup and raise the heat to high.

Cut up the chicken on a separate cutting board from the one you cut up the vegetables on. Cut the chicken tenders into 1-inch pieces across and add them to the stew. Wash up right away with lots of soap and hot water so that the raw chicken doesn't get on anything else in the kitchen or any other food.

When the stew comes up to a boil again, add the ravioli and leave the lid off. Cook stew until the ravioli is almost done, about 5 minutes. Turn off the heat and let the stew cool down a little bit. Serve up the stew and pass cheese and bread at the table to go with it.

CHICKEN RAVIOLI

1 servings
Source: Ravioli Greats

4 cups **sifted flour**

½ **teapoon salt**

5 **eggs**

¼ cup **warm water, (625 ml)**

chicken filling

2 cups **cooked chicken, chopped**

1 **egg**

½ cup **grated parmesan, (60g) cheese**

1 tablespoon **minced parsley**

1 cup **cooked spinach, chopped**

salt and pepper

Sift flour onto a large pastry board. Make a well in the center and add salt, eggs, and water. Mix thoroughly. Knead the dough for about two minutes. Allow dough to stand for ten minutes.

Divide the dough into quantities that are easy to roll out. Roll each section out on a floured flour to a thickness of 1/8 inch (3mm), Cut into 2 inch (5cm) rounds or squares and place a teaspoon of filling the center.

Cover with another circle or square and press edges together with a fork. Cook in boiling salted water until dough is tender. Serve with sauce of your choice.

CHOCOLATE-FILLED RAVIOLI COOKIE

48 servings
Source: Ravioli Greats

1 cup **sugar**

½ cup **shortening**

¼ cup **margarine or butter, softened**

2 **eggs**

1 teaspoon **vanilla**

2 ½ cups **all-purpose flour***

1 teaspoon **baking soda**

½ teaspoon **salt**

¾ cups **miniature chocolate chips**

¾ cups **walnuts**

honey

finely chopped walnuts

***If using self-rising flour, omit baking soda and salt. rease flour to 2 ⅓ cups.**

Mix sugar, shortening, margarine, eggs and vanilla. Stir in flour, baking soda and salt. Divide dough into 4 equal parts. Cover and refrigerate 2 hours. Place chocolate chips and walnuts in blender or food processor. Cover and blend, or process, about 30 seconds, or until mixture begins to hold together. Heat oven to 400°F.

Roll one part of dough into rectangle, 12 X 8 inches, on lightly floured surface. Cut dough into 12 rectangles, each 3 X inches. Place 1 teaspoon packed chocolate mixture on one end of each rectangle. Using metal spatula or knife dipped into flour, carefully fold dough over filling. Pinch edges to seal.

Press edges with fork dipped into flour. Place on ungreased cookie sheet. Bake 8 to 10 minutes or until cookies are light brown. Brush warm cookies with honey. Sprinkle with finely chopped nuts. Remove to rack to cool. Repeat with remaining dough. DOZEN COOKIES; 100 CALORIES PER COOKIE.

Author Note: average

DUCK CONFIT AND MASHED POTATO RAVIOLI W WHITE TRUFFLE SAUCE

6 servings
Source: Ravioli Greats

- 2 **russet potatoes, about 1 pound**
- 2 tablespoons **sour cream**
- 14 ounces **confit of duck leg, 2 whole legs***
- 3 tablespoons **unsalted butter**
- 1 **garlic clove, minced**
- 56 **wonton wrappers, thawed if frozen**
- 28 **flat leafed parsley**
- 2 tablespoons **white truffle oil****
- 2 tablespoons **white truffle paste,**
- optional **
- *****GARNISH*****
- **flat leafed parsley leaves**

Peel and quarter potatoes and in a saucepan combine with enough cold water to cover by 2-inches. Simmer potatoes 15 to 20 minutes, or until soft, and drain in a colander. Return potatoes to pan and steam, covered, over moderate heat, shaking pan, 30 seconds to evaporate any excess liquid. Force hot potatoes through a ricer or medium disk of a food mill into a bowl and beat in sour cream and salt and pepper to taste.

Remove skin from duck legs and cut into 1/4-inch strips. In a small heavy skillet cook skin in 1 tablespoon butter over moderately low heat, stirring occasionally, until crisp and transfer cracklings with a slotted spoon to paper towels to drain.

Remove meat from duck legs and chop fine. Add garlic to fat

Chapter 1: A–M

remaining in skillet and cook over moderately low heat, stirring occasionally, until softened. Add meat to skillet and cook over moderate heat, stirring occasionally, until heated through. Stir in salt and pepper to taste. Stir meat mixture into potato mixture and cool. Filling may be made 1 day ahead and chilled, covered.

Put 1 wrapper on a lightly floured surface and mound 1 tablespoon filling in center. Top filling with 1 parsley leaf. Lightly brush edges of wrapper with water and put a second wrapper over first, pressing down around filling to force out air and sealing edges well. Trim excess dough with a round cutter or sharp knife. Make more ravioli with remaining wrappers, filling, and parsley in same manner, transferring as formed to a dry kitchen towel and turning occasionally to dry slightly.

In a kettle of gently boiling salted water cook ravioli in 2 batches 2 minutes, or until they rise to surface and are tender. Do not let water boil vigorously once ravioli have been added. Transfer ravioli as cooked with a slotted spoon to a dry kitchen towel to drain and keep warm.

While ravioli are cooking, in the small heavy skillet cook remaining 2 tablespoons butter over moderate heat, swirling skillet occasionally, until nut brown in color. Remove skillet from heat and stir in truffle oil and paste.

Arrange 4 or 5 ravioli on each of 6 heated plates and spoon truffle sauce on top. Garnish each serving with cracklings and parsley leaves.

EASY CHICKEN RAVIOLI

4 servings
Source: Ravioli Greats

6 ounces **ground raw chicken or turkey**

1 8 oz contain soft-style **cream cheese with chives and onion**

Ravioli Greats

¼ cup **shredded carrot**
20 / " **wonton wrappers**
1 tablespoon **cooking oil**

marinara sauce or spaghetti sauce, warmed

Stir together chicken or turkey, cream cheese, and carrot in a medium mixing bowl; set aside.

Place about 1 Tbsp of filling in the center of each wrapper. Brush edges with water. Fold one corner over to the opposite corner, forming a triangle. To seal, press edges together or use a pastry wheel.

Bring a large amount of water and the cooking oil to boiling in a Dutch oven. Drop ravioli into the water. Reduce heat and simmer, uncovered, for 3 to 4 minutes or till no pink remains in the chicken or turkey. Remove ravioli with a slotted spoon. Drain on paper towels. Divide ravioli among 4 serving plates. Ladle warm sauce over ravioli.

To freeze, place uncooked ravioli in a freezer container; seal, label, and freeze for up to 3 months. To cook frozen ravioli, drop into boiling water as directed above, cooking for 5-6 minutes.

EGGPLANT-FILLED RAVIOLI WITH TOMATO CREAM SAUCE

6 servings
Source: Ravioli Greats

FILLING

1 **medium eggplant**

salt

2 tablespoons **olive oil**

1 **small onion, chopped**

2 cups **garlic, minced**

2 tablespoons **white wine, dry**

2 tablespoons **parsley; fresh, minced**

1 tablespoon **basil; fresh, minced or 1 t dried, crumbled**

freshly ground pepper

PASTA

Chapter 1: A–M

3 cups **flour, all-purpose**

3 **eggs**

½ teaspoon **salt**

3 tablespoons **water, (about)**

*****SAUCE*****

½ cup **madeira**

¼ cup **white wine, dry**

3 tablespoons **shallots, minced**

2 cups **whipping cream**

¼ teaspoon **lemon peel, grated**

1 cup **tomatoes; Italian plum, peel**

seeded and chopped

OR drained chopped

canned it, alian plum tomatoes

minced fresh basil

FOR FILLING: Peel eggplant and slice 1/2-inch thick. Salt generously on both sides. Drain on paper towels 45 minutes. Pat dry with paper towels. Cut eggplant into 1/2-inch cubes. Heat oil in heavy large skillet over medium heat. Add onion and garlic and Saute until soft, about 5 minutes. Add eggplant and Saute until beginning to turn golden brown, about 15 minutes. Stir in wine, parsley and basil, scraping up browned bits. Cover and cook until eggplant is tender, about 3 minutes. Season with salt and pepper. Transfer to processor or blender and puree until smooth. Cool completely.

FOR PASTA: Combine flour, eggs and salt in processor and mix well. With machine running, add just enough water through feed tube to form ball. Remove from processor. Cover dough and let rest for 30 minutes. (Pasta dough can also be made by hand.) Cut dough into 4 pieces. Flatten 1 piece (keep remainder covered), then fold in thirds. Turn pasta machine to widest setting and run dough through several times until smooth and velvety, folding before each run and dusting with flour if sticky. Adjust machine to next narrower setting. Run dough through machine without folding. Repeat, narrowing rollers after each run, until pasta is 1/16 to 1/8-inch thick, dusting with flour as necessary. Line baking sheets with towels. Set sheet of dough on work surface. Place about 1-1/2 teaspoons filling at 2-inch intervals along sheet. Roll second piece of dough. Set atop first sheet. Press down around filling to force out air and seal dough. Cut into 2-inch squares. Arrange on prepared sheets. Repeat with remaining dough and filling. Cover with towel.

FOR SAUCE: Combine Madeira, wine and shallots in heavy small saucepan. Boil until reduced to 1/4 cup, about 4 minutes. Add cream and peel and boil 5 minutes, stirring occasionally. Stir in tomatoes. Season with salt and pepper. Cook ravioli in large pot of boiling water until just tender but still firm to bite, about 4 minutes for fresh. Remove with slotted spoon; drain. Divide among plates. Spoon sauce over. Garnish with basil. Serve immediately.

DO AHEAD HINTS: * Ravioli can be prepared one day ahead and refrigerated or one month ahead, wrapped tightly and frozen. Do not thaw before cooking. * Sauce can be prepared one day ahead; refrigerate. EVEN EASIER: * Purchase sheets of fresh pasta for the ravioli or buy prepared ravioli to serve with the tomato cream sauce here.

FILO RAVIOLI WITH APPLES AND PEARS

6 servings
Source: Ravioli Greats

=== **CARAMELIZED WALNUTS** ===

1 cup **sugar**

½ cup **water**

½ cup **walnuts, chopped**

=== **FILLING** ===

1 **baking apple, peeled, cored, and diced**

2 **pears, peeled, cored, and diced**

1 ½ cups **Pinot Noir**

2 cups **brown sugar – (lightly packed)**

½ **cinnamon stick**

¼ cup **butter, room temperature**

1 teaspoon **cinnamon**

1 teaspoon **ground allspice**

⅛ teaspoon **salt**

¼ cup **blueberry syrup**

=== **ASSEMBLY** ===

8 sheets **filo, thawed**

½ cup **butter, melted**

For the Caramelized Walnuts: Combine sugar and water in small saucepan over high heat and cook until sugar is dissolved, boiling 5 minutes. Add walnuts and toss. Remove nuts with slotted spoon to baking sheet to cool.

For the Filling: Combine apple, pears, wine, 1 cup brown sugar and cinnamon stick in saucepan. Bring to simmer over medium heat and poach until fruit is tender, 10 minutes.

Remove apple and pears to bowl using slotted spoon. Continue cooking liquid until reduced by 1/2 and thickened like syrup, 5 minutes. Set aside to serve with Ravioli.

Add Caramelized Walnuts, butter, remaining brown sugar, cinnamon, allspice, salt and syrup to fruit mixture and toss lightly until combined.

To Assemble: Brush filo with melted butter and separate in 2 stacks. Set 1 stack aside. Place small mounds of fruit mixture evenly on filo in 2 rows of 3.

Lay second stack of filo sheets on top. Seal ends of filo with melted butter. Using pizza cutter or ravioli cutter, cut evenly into 6 squares.

Place squares on baking sheet lined with parchment paper and bake at 400 degrees until ravioli are golden brown, 12 to 15 minutes. Serve with reserved Pinot Noir syrup.

This recipe yields 6 servings.

Each serving: 861 calories; 412 mg sodium; 62 mg cholesterol; 30 grams fat; 143 grams carbohydrates; 5 grams protein; 1.41 grams fiber.

FRIED RAVIOLI

6 servings
Source: Ravioli Greats

1 egg

2 tablespoons **water**

½ cup **fine dry bread crumbs**

2 tablespoons **parmesan cheese**

½ teaspoon **dried oregano leaves, crush**

14 ounces **ravioli; frozen, thawed**

meat –or– cheese filled

vegetable oil for frying

2 cups **spaghetti sauce**

In small bowl, with fork, beat together egg and water; set aside.

In another small bowl, stir together bread crumbs, parmesan cheese and oregano. Dip each ravioli into egg mix and then coat with crumb mix.

In 10" skillet, heat 1/2" oil to 375°F

Cook ravioli, a few at a time, 1 minute each side or until golden. Drain on paper towels. Repeat with remaining raviolis.

Meanwhile, heat spaghetti sauce until hot. Spoon sauce onto center of serving platter. Arrange ravioli on top of sauce.

HAZELNUT SQUASH RAVIOLI FILLING

3 servings
Source: Ravioli Greats

1 **small butternut squash**

½ cup **hazelnuts**

1 cup **onions, diced**

1 teaspoon **garlic, minced**

1 tablespoon **olive oil**

½ cup **breadcrumbs**

Preheat oven to 350°F.

Cut squash into quarters, remove seeds & place in a baking dish with 1/2 c water. Cover & bake till tender.

Cool & then scrape out the flesh & mash. Set aside.

Increase oven temperature to 375°F.

Place hazelnuts on a cookie sheet & roast until lightly browned, about 7 minutes. Let cool & then rub off their skins.

Saute onion & garlic in oil until browned. Add 1 c squash & cook for 2 minutes over medium heat.

Place all ingredients in a food processor & process until smooth.

Use to fill pasta dough of your choice & cook as desired.

HERBAL RAVIOLI ON POACHED TOMATOES AND BASIL

4 servings
Source: Ravioli Greats

- 2 8.5x11" **fresh pasta sheets**
- 1 ¼ cups **ricotta cheese, fat free**
- ¾ cups **Italian bread crumbs**
- ¼ cup **fresh basil, chopped**
- ¼ cup **fresh parsley, chopped**
- ⅛ teaspoon **dried oregano**
- ⅛ teaspoon **nutmeg**
- ⅛ teaspoon **salt**
- ⅛ teaspoon **black pepper, freshly ground**
- 3 qt **boiling water**

poached tomato base
- 2 large **tomatoes, ripe**
- 2 cloves **garlic, thinly sliced**
- 6 **fresh basil leaves**
- ¼ cup **water**
- ⅛ teaspoon **salt**

Purchase or prepare pasta. Set aside.

In large mixing bowl, combine ricotta, bread crumbs, basil, parsley, oregano, nutmeg, salt and black pepper. Mix well. Set aside. Makes about 2 cups of stuffing.

Lay pasta sheets flat on work surface and drop four equal portions (about 1/4 cup) of ricotta mixture onto the 4 quadrants on the left half only of each sheet of pasta. Slightly wet the outer rim of both pasta sheets with water. Fold right half of pasta sheet over other half. Press down around each cheese mound to seal.

Use a pasta cutter to further seal and crimp edges, dividing pasta packets into 8 squares (or fill 16 to 20 ravioli, 2" x 2" with 1 heaping tablespoon of stuffing each.)

Bring water to boil in large pot. Drop ravioli into water and boil 3-5 minutes, or until they float. Carefully remove and drain ravioli. Do not let them touch while drying or the will stick together.

Wash, core, peel and rough-chop tomatoes. Set aside. Briefly saute garlic in a non-stick saute pan over medium heat. Add tomatoes, basil, water and salt. Cover and cook 5 minutes or until mixture cooks down to form a tomato sauce. Makes about 1 1/2 cups sauce.

Spoon tomato mixture onto 4 serving plates and top each plate with two ravioli.

Makes 4 large servings.

INSIDE OUT RAVIOLI

8 servings
Source: Ravioli Greats

1 lb. **ground beef, uncooked**   1 jar spaghetti sauce, (32 oz.)

1 cup **longhorn cheese, grated**

½ cup **romano cheese, grated**

1 cup **mozzarella cheese, grated**

3 cups **medium shells, uncooked**

1 **package frozen chopped spinach, (10 oz.)**

½ cup **oil**

Thaw and drain moisture from spinach. Combine all ingredients, except mozzarella cheese in bowl and mix to combine.

Pour into 9x13 inch pan and top with mozzarella cheese. Bake in a 350°F oven for 45 minutes to 1 hour.

INSIDE OUT RAVIOLI - 1

6 servings
Source: Ravioli Greats

1 lb. **lean ground beef**

salt and pepper to taste

1 **medium onion, chopped**

6 ounces **mastoccioli pasta**

3 cloves **garlic**

10 ounces **spinach; frozen, cooked**

1 tablespoon **salad oil, (opt)**

1 cup **american cheese, grated**

16 ounces **tomato sauce**

½ cup **soft bread crumbs**

6 ounces **tomato paste**

2 **eggs, well beaten**

1 tablespoon **dried parsley**

¼ cup **salad oil**

½ teaspoon **oregano**

¼ cup **parmesan cheese, grated**

Brown meat, onion and garlic in oil (oil is optional for use if meat is extra-lean). Drain excess grease.

Add tomato sauce and paste (diluted with 3 cans of water), dried parsley, oregano, salt and pepper.

Ravioli Greats

Simmer for 10 minutes Cook the mostaccioli as directed on package. Drain and rinse with cold water.

Put back into pan in which it was cooked. Add cooked spinach, American cheese, bread crumbs, eggs, oil and parmesan cheese.

Spread mixture in a 9x13" greased baking dish. Top with meat mixture. Sprinkle more grated parmesan cheese on top.

Bake at 350°F for 30 minutes.

INSIDE OUT RAVIOLI - 2

12 servings
Source: Ravioli Greats

1 **package**
spinach, frozen-chopped (10

1 tablespoon **oil**

1 lb. **ground beef**

1 medium **onion-chopped**

1 **garlic, cloves/minced**

1 lb. **spaghetti sauce with mushroom**

1 cup **tomato sauce, (8oz)**

½ teaspoon **salt**

⅛ teaspoon **pepper**

2 cups **macaroni-cooked**

1 cup **cheddar cheese-shredded**

½ cup **bread crumbs-soft**

2 **eggs-well beaten**

¼ cup **oil**

Cook spinach according to package directions – drain, reserving liquid. Add water to make I cup; set aside. Heat I tbsp. oil on medium high heat. Saute beef, onions and garlic.

When lightly brown, add spinach liquid, spaghetti sauce, tomato sauce, salt and pepper. Simmer for 10 minutes.

Preheat oven to 350°F.

Combine spinach, macaroni, cheese, bread crumbs, eggs, 1/4 c. oil. Pour this mixture into a greased 13x9x2 inch baking dish (I use two smaller round dishes in order to freeze one). Top with meat sauce.

Bake for 30 minutes.

LAMB SPIRALS WITH GOAT CHEESE RAVIOLI

4 servings
Source: Ravioli Greats

- 4 four-ounce **Lamb Paillardes (5"x5"x1/8"), See Directions**
- ⅛ cup **garlic, roasted**
- ⅛ cup **pine nuts, roasted**
- 2 tablespoons **olive oil**
- 4 pieces **string**
- 1 pinch **salt, to taste**
- 1 pinch **fresh ground black pepper, to taste**
- 32 **won-ton wrappers**
- 1 cup **goat cheese**
- 1 tablespoon **fresh Italian parsley, chopped**
- 1 pinch **fresh ground black pepper**
- ½ cup **veal glaze**
- 1 tablespoon **fresh savory, chopped**
- 1 tablespoon **pink peppercorns**
- 2 cups **beurre blanc, See Recipe**

CHEF'S NOTE: A "paillarde" is a piece of meat that has been pounded flat before cooking.

STEP ONE: Prepare the Lamb--

Prepare each paillarde of lamb by pounding a 4-ounce portion between waxed paper until 5-inches by 5-inches by 1/8 inch thick.

Place the lamb pieces flat on a cutting board. Mix roasted garlic with roasted pine nuts and 2 tablespoons of olive oil in a blender until

Ravioli Greats

smooth. Season with a pinch of salt and pepper and spread evenly on lamb. Roll the lamb into spirals, making four separate portions. Tie the string around the lamb to hold the spiral in shape. Season and set aside.

STEP TWO: Prepare the Ravioli--

Mix goat cheese with Italian parsley and a pinch of pepper. Place a dab of cheese mixture into the center of the wonton wrapper. Wet the edges of the wrapper, fold and securely pinch the edges together.

STEP THREE: Prepare the Beurre Blanc--

STEP FOUR: Final Assembly--

Charbroil the lamb spirals to Medium Rare. Remove string and slice into 20 pieces (5 slices per lamb spiral). Cook the ravioli in boiling water until done. Toss ravioli with Beurre Blanc and place in center of four plates. Place five lamb spirals around inner rim of each plate, sauce the meat with veal glaze, and garnish the ravioli with savory and pink peppercorns and serve.

LEMONY CHICKEN & ANCHOVY RAVIOLI

4 servings
Source: Ravioli Greats

2 teaspoons **olive oil**

250 g **minced chicken**

4 **anchovy fillets, chopped**

2 tablespoons **grated fresh parmesan cheese**

1 tablespoon **cream**

¼ teaspoon **ground nutmeg**

1 teaspoon **grated lemon rind**

2 tablespoons **lemon juice**

¼ cup **chopped fresh parsley**

1 quantity **plain pasta dough**

(2 cups flour, 3 eggs)

60 g **fresh parmesan cheese thinly sliced, (optional)**

CREAMY CHEESE SAUCE

30 g **butter**

2 tablespoons **plain flour**

1 cup **water**

1 **small chicken stock cube, crumbled**

1 300 **millilit cream**

2 tablespoons **grated fresh parmesan cheese**

Heat oil in pan, add chicken, cook, stirring for 2 minutes. Stir in anchovies, cheese, cream, nutmeg, rind, juice and parsley. Blend or process mixture until smooth.

Divide pasta dough in half, roll each piece until 2 mm thick. Place 1/4 level Tsp of filling 3 cm apart over 1 sheet of pasta. Lightly brush remaining pasta sheet with water, place over filling; press firmly between filling. Cut into square ravioli shapes. Lightly sprinkle ravioli with a little flour.

Just before serving, add ravioli to large pan of boiling water, boil,uncovered, for about 5 minutes or until just tender; drain. Combine ravioli with hot sauce; serve topped with extra cheese.

Creamy Cheese Sauce: Melt butter in pan, add flour; stir over heat until bubbling. Remove from heat, gradually stir in combined water and stock cube, stir over heat until mixture boils and thickens. Simmer,uncovered, until reduced by half. Just before serving, stir in cream and cheese. Serves 4.

MOCK RAVIOLI

1 servings
Source: Ravioli Greats

--meat mixture---

1 large garlic clove, minced

1 can tomato paste

2 medium onions, finely chopped

¾ teaspoons **rosemary**

1 cup **water**

Ravioli Greats

- ¾ teaspoons **oregano**
- 2 lbs. **beef ground**
- 1 cup **parmesan cheese, divided**
- 1 can **tomato sauce**
- 1 cup **parsley; chopped, divided** ---spinach layer---
- 1 cup **vegetable oil**
- 1 teaspoon **garlic salt**
- 4 packages **spinach, frozen, chopped**
- 1 teaspoon **ground sage**
- 6 **eggs, well beaten**
- 1 lb. **butterfly macaroni**
- 2 cups **bread crumbs soft**

Saute onions, minced garlic and meat. Add 1/3 cup parsley and 1/3 cup parmesan cheese and remaining meat mixture ingredients and simmer. For spinach layer combine oil, 1/3 cup parsley, spinach, bread crumbs, 1/3 cup parmesan cheese, eggs and 1 tsp garlic salt and 1 tsp ground sage.

Cook pasta and drain well. Sprinkle 1/3 cup parsley and 1/3 cup Parmesan cheese over pasta and mix well. Butter a large baking dish. Cover the bottom with a layer of pasta, then a layer of the spinach mix, then a layer of meat. Repeat layers until all ingredients are used, ending with the meat sauce.

Sprinkle remaining parmesan cheese and parsley over top. Bake at 350°F for 20-30 minutes.

Chapter 2
N–Z

PANSOTTI TRIANGLES WITH ARTICHOKES LIKE GENOA'S

4 servings
Source: Ravioli Greats

--filling---

2 ounces **artichoke hearts, fresh or thawed**

¼ cup **ricotta cheese**

2 tablespoons **mascarpone cheese**

½ cup **grated parmesan cheese**

1 teaspoon **arugula leaves, (rocket), minced**

1 teaspoon **fresh flat-leaf parsley,** minced

¼ teaspoon **minced garlic**

salt and pepper

freshly ground nutmeg

½ lb. **pasta, cut in 2" squares -** sauce---

¼ cup **unsalted butter**

½ cup **chopped artichoke hearts,** steamed

2 tablespoons **chopped fresh herbs**

¼ cup **arugula leaves, (rocket)**

salt and pepper

Prepare frozen artichoke hearts according to package directions. Recipe calls for 4 to 5 ounces total but only 2 ounces are needed for the soft-cheese filling.

Make FILLING the day before. In a food processor fitted with a metal blade, puree 2 ounces of artichokes and ricotta cheese until smooth. In a bowl, combine the puree, mascarpone and parmesan, argula,

24

parsley and garlic. Mix well. Refrigerate over night.

Select fresh herbs, one or a mixture: parsley, basil, thyme, marjoram, sage, chives

Cut 2" squares from the pasta. Fill each square with 1/2 to 1 teaspoon of the filling. Fold the pasta over to form a triangle. Use water to hold edge. Place in a single layer on a rack until slightly dry to the the touch (1 to 2 hours). The pasta will cook in 2 to 3 minutes.

Make the sauce. In a large frying pan over low heat, melt the butter. Add chopped artichoke hearts and saute until heated through, about 1 minutes. Drain the pasta briefly in a colander and immediately add it to the artichokes. Raise the heat to high and toss the pasta gently. Add the hearts and arugula and toss again until mixed. Season and serve

Author Note: Pansotti Genovesi con Carciofi An idea from the Ligurian coast on the Gulf of Genoa in northwestern Italy where herbs are plentiful. Fill pasta with soft cheese, artichokes and herbs. Shape the ravioli into triangles. Make a butter sauce with artichokes and herbs.

PERFECT SAFFRON PASTA

4 servings
Source: Ravioli Greats

Makes about 2/3 pound, 4 to 6 servings.

The rich flavor and aroma of this pasta are wonderful with fish and shellfish in a broth, wine, or cream sauce, or with sauteed chicken. It stands up well to sauces that have the strong flavor of olives and acid ingredients such as wine and tomatoes. Try Saffron Pasta with sweet peppers, garlic, and onions or leeks. Here, we shape it into bow ties, called farfalle ("butterflies") in Italian.

teaspoons saffron threads, firmly packed 1 tablespoon hot water 2 cups unbleached flour 2 extra-large eggs

In a small bowl, combine the saffron and the water and let stand 10 minutes. If you are making the pasta by hand, add the saffron and water to the eggs after you have beaten them lightly with a fork. If you are making the pasta in a food processor, add the saffron water to the work bowl after you have added the eggs.

After rolling the dough through the next-to-last setting on the pasta machine, cut it into 1-by-2-inch rectangles with a fluted ravioli cutter or knife. With your thumb and forefinger, pinch the centers of the rectangles together to make bow ties and set them on tea towels or a lightly floured surface.

FETA, CHIVES & PISTACHIOS W/ SAFFRON PASTA

Serves 4 to 6.

Bright and beautiful, golden bow ties are dressed with chopped chives and pistachios. Serve them as a side dish or a light but satisfying main course.

Water 6 ounces feta cheese, crumbled 1/3 cup roasted, shelled, and peeled pistachios, coarsely chopped 1/3 cup chopped Chives 3 tablespoons currants, softened in hot water and drained 2 tablespoons extra-virgin olive oil Salt 1 batch Saffron Pasta Freshly ground black pepper

In a large pot, bring several quarts of water to a boil. Meanwhile, place the cheese, pistachios, chives, currants, and olive oil in a large saute pan.

When the water comes to a boil, salt it well, add the pasta, and cook it al dente. Drain it, reserving about 1/2 cup of the cooking water. Add the drained pasta to the saute pan along with enough of the reserved cooking water to make a sauce that just coats the noodles. Season with salt and pepper and toss well. If desired, you may drizzle the top lightly with olive oil. Serve hot.

POPPY SEED RAVIOLI COOKIES

48 servings
Source: Ravioli Greats

1 cup **Sugar**

½ cup **Shortening**

¼ cup **Margarine or butter**

softened

2 **Eggs**

1 teaspoon **Vanilla**

2 ½ cups **All-purpose flour***

1 teaspoon **Baking soda**

½ teaspoon **Salt**

½ cup **Poppy seed**

½ cup **Almonds**

½ cup **Milk**

2 tablespoons **Honey**

1 teaspoon **Finely shredded lemon peel**

1 tablespoon **Lemon juice**

Honey

Poppy seed

*if using self-rising flour - omit Baking soda and salt.

rease

Flour to

2 ⅓ **Cups.**

Mix sugar, shortening, margarine, eggs and vanilla. Stir in flour, baking soda and salt. Divide dough into 4 equal parts. Cover and refrigerate 2 hours. Place 1/2 cup poppy seed, the almonds, milk, 2 tablespoons honey, the lemon peel and lemon juice in blender or food processor.

Cover and blend, or process, until liquid is absorbed. Heat oven to 400°F. Roll one part of dough into rectangle, 12 X 8 inches, on lightly floured surface.

Cut dough into 12 rectangles, each 3 X inches. Place 1 teaspoon poppy seed mixture on one end of each rectangle. Using metal spatula or knife dipped into flour, carefully fold dough over filling. Pinch edges to seal.

Press edges with fork dipped into flour. Place on ungreased cookie sheet. Bake 8 to 10 minutes or until cookies are light brown. Brush warm cookies with honey. Sprinkle with poppy seed. Remove to rack to cool. Repeat with remaining dough.

4 DOZEN COOKIES; 95 CALORIES PER COOKIE.

POTATO RAVIOLI WITH BUTTER SAGE

4 servings
Source: Ravioli Greats

1 recipe green pasta, see * note

2 tablespoons salt

=== **filling** ===

4 large russet potatoes, baked until soft, peeled and mashed

½ cup **grated pecorino-romano cheese, divided**

¼ cup **extra-virgin olive oil**

1 large egg -, (extra-large), lightly beaten

4 scallions, sliced thinly

1 pn grated nutmeg

salt, to taste

freshly-ground black pepper, to taste

=== **sauce** ===

6 ounces unsalted butter

8 perfect fresh sage leaves

To prepare the pasta: Roll the Green Pasta dough into 4 sheets on the thinnest setting. Take one sheet of pasta and place on a lightly-floured cutting board. Cut each sheet into thirds lengthwise, then score each length in half and in half again yielding four 3-inch squares. Cover with a towel.

To make the filling: In a large mixing bowl, place the mashed potatoes, 1/4 cup of the Pecorino-Romano cheese, olive oil, egg, scallions, nutmeg and salt and pepper. Mix together until well incorporated. Set aside.

To assemble the ravioli: Into each square place 1 scant tablespoon filling. Fold opposing corners together to form a triangular pillow (remember to gently press out any air between the filling and the pasta dough). If the pasta is a little dry, moisten the edges with a little water to help it adhere. Be certain to seal the ravioli well on both flat sides or it will burst while cooking. Repeat with the remaining sheets of green pasta. Continue until pasta is all filled. At the half way point, check to be sure that you're halfway in using the filling. If not, adjust the quantity of filling for the remainder of pasta.

Bring 6 quarts water to a boil and add 2 tablespoons salt.

To make the sauce: Melt the butter and sage at the same time over medium heat until just starting to bubble, set aside. Gently drop the raviolis into boiling water and cook 3 to 4 minutes on a low boil, until the pasta is cooked through. Remove from water with a slotted spoon and place into pan with butter and sage. Simmer for 1 minute over low heat. Sprinkle with remaining Pecorino cheese. Place into a warm serving platter.

POTSTICKERS - 1

2 servings
Source: Ravioli Greats

dough

2 cups **flour, all-purpose**

½ cup **water**

filling

½ lb. **pork, ground**

½ **small Chinese, (Napa), cabbage, cored**

chopped

1 green onion, coarsely chopped

2 ginger, (fresh), thumb-sized slices,

2 water chestnuts, chopped

1 teaspoon **salt**

½ teaspoon **sugar**

1 **pn white pepper**

1 teaspoon **sesame oil**

*****TO COOK*****

5 tablespoons **vegetable oil**

1 cup **water**

*****sauce*****

hot chili oil

red rice vinegar

soy sauce

In a bowl, combine flour and water, mixing to form a ball. Remove to a floured board and knead with your palm for about 3 minutes. Shape into a ball, cover with a damp towel, and let stand for about 10 minutes.

Make the filling by combining the filling ingredients above. Refrigerate until ready to use.

To shape and assemble, knead dough for about 3 minutes. Roll into a cylinder that is about 1 inch in diameter. Cut off the ends, then cut into about 24 pieces, each about 3/4-inch wide. With the cut side up, press the dough down with your palm to flatten. Use a rolling pin to make pancakes about 2 1/2 - 3 inches in diameter. (They get quite thin; that's what you want.) Spoon about 1 tablespoon of filling into the center of each pancake. Fold the dough over to make a half circle and pleat the edges firmly together.

To pan-fry, heat cast-iron or other heavy-bottom skillet over moderate heat. Add about 3 T oil, swirling to coat bottom. (Watch out, it sizzles quite a bit. Don't get burned!) When oil is hot, place potstickers, seam side up, in skillet and agitate (shake) for 30 seconds. Pour in water, cover and gently boil over moderate heat for 7 to 8 minutes. When oil and water start to sizzle, add remaining 2 T oil. Tip skillet to distribute oil evenly; watch carefully (uncovered) to prevent sticking. When bottoms are brown (usually several minutes later), remove from heat and carefully lift out potstickers with spatula.

To serve, turn potstickers over (dark side up) and arrange on serving platter. Combine chili oil, vinegar and soy sauce in proportions to suit your taste and offer sauce for dipping. Alternatively, cut up a hot chili pepper into red rice vinegar.

Notes:

* You can freeze uncooked potstickers for later use, if you squeeze out the water from the cabbage during preparation (in a colander or cheesecloth). Freeze potstickers separately on cookie sheets until firm, then put them in plastic bags. When rolling out the pancakes, leave the centers slightly thicker than the edges. A thicker center will hold up better during the browning.

* If you prefer, steam potstickers for about 12 minutes over boiling water instead of pan-frying. (No self-respecting hacker would be caught eating steamed potstickers, though.)

* These are really not hard to make, and come out quite nicely! Following the dough recipe above leads to a fairly dry and floury dough; this makes it hard to roll out and pleat. Feel free to add a little more water. There are also now commercially available potsticker presses that take care of folding and pleating; they're cheap and plastic and work rather well.

* The perfect potsticker is uniformly brown with a thick brown area on the bottom (where it sticks to the pot); it seems that achieving this only comes with practice. I tend to fry both sides a bit before adding the water; this helps. Beware of too much heat; the bottom will bubble and crack. This doesn't taste any different, but doesn't look as nice.

* If you don't cook the whole batch at once, store the potstickers so that they don't touch; the dough tends to stick to itself, so the potstickers may tear as you remove them.

Chapter 2: N–Z

* Many restaurants serve Hoy Sin sauce (hoisin) instead of hot sauce.

PUMPKIN RAVIOLI

6 servings
Source: Ravioli Greats

1 cup **Ricotta Cheese**
½ cup **Pumpkin, Canned**
½ teaspoon **Salt**
¼ teaspoon **Nutmeg, Ground**
2 cups **Unbleached Flour**
½ teaspoon **Salt**

¼ cup **Tomato Paste**
1 tablespoon **Olive Or Vegetable Oil**
2 **Eggs, Large**
Pumpkin Seed Sauce

Mix the cheese, pumpkin, 1/2 tsp salt and the nutmeg. Set aside. Mix the flour, and 1/2 tsp salt in a large bowl. Make a well in the center of the flour. Beat the tomato paste, oil and eggs until well blended and pour into the well in the flour. Stir with a fork gradually bring the flour mixture to the center of the bowl.

Do this until the dough makes a ball. If the dough is too dry, mix in up to 2 tbls of water. Knead lightly on a floured cloth-covered surface, adding flour if dough is sticky, until smooth and elastic, about 5 minutes. Cover and let rest for another 5 minutes. Divide the dough into 4 equal parts. Roll the dough, one part at a time, into a rectangle about 12 X 10-inches. (Keep the rest of the dough covered.)

Drop the pumpkin mixture by 2 level tsps onto half of the rectangle, about 1 1/2-inches apart in 2 rows of 4 mounds each. Moisten the edges of the dough and the dough between the rows of pumpkin mixture with water. Fold the other half of the dough up over the pumpkin mixture, pressing the dough down around the pumpkin.

Trim the edges with a pastry wheel or knife.

Cut between the rows of filling to make ravioli; press the edges together with a fork or cut with a pastry wheel sealing the edges well. Repeat with the remaining dough and pumpkin filling. Place ravioli on towel, let stand turning once, until dry, about 30 minutes. Prepare the Pumpkin Seed Sauce. Heat until hot; reserve keeping it warm. Cook ravioli in 4 quarts of boiling salted water (2 tsp of salt) until tender, about 10 to 15 minutes; drain carefully. Serve the ravioli with the warm Pumpkin Seed Sauce spooned over.

PUMPKIN RAVIOLI IN CHICKEN BROTH

4 servings
Source: Ravioli Greats

*****for ravioli*****

1 lb. **roasted pumpkin flesh***

½ cup **grated parmesan cheese**

2 teaspoons **freshly chopped sage**

salt and pepper to taste

16 won ton wrappers, thawed if frozen

1 ⅓ cups **good quality chicken stock**

*****for garnish*****

2 tablespoons **toasted pine nuts**

chopped sage leaves

coarsely grated parmesan cheese

*To roast the pumpkin, preheat oven to 400°F. Cut the pumpkin in half, scrape out seeds and string, and place cut side down in a roasting pan. Roast until very tender, about 1 hour. When done, scrape out roasted flesh and set aside 1 pound.

To make the filling, combine in a blender the roasted pumpkin, 1/3 cup of grated Parmesan, and sage. Puree until smooth. Check for consistency and taste. If needed, add the remaining

Parmesan. Season to taste with salt and pepper and cool.

Bring a kettle of salted water to a gentle boil for the ravioli.

Put 1 wrapper on a lightly floured surface and mound 1 level tablespoon filling in center. Brush edges of wrapper with water and fold wrapper in half to form a triangle, pressing around filling to force out air. Transfer ravioli to a dry kitchen towel to drain. Make more ravioli with remaining wrappers and filling in same manner, transferring to towel and turning occasionally to dry slightly.

Cook ravioli in gently boiling water in 2 batches 6 to 8 minutes, or until they rise to surface and are tender. Do not let water boil vigorously once ravioli have been added. With a spoon transfer ravioli to a paper towel lined plate to drain.

In a saucepan, heat the chicken stock until simmering. Ladle about 1/3 cup of stock into 4 individual serving dishes, divide the ravioli and garnish with toasted pine nuts, freshly chopped sage and coarsely grated Parmesan.

PURIM RAVIOLI

1 servings
Source: Ravioli Greats

2 lbs. **Spinach;small leaves bulk Salt**

2 tablespoons **Olive oil**

1 **Onion;small, quartered**

1 **Carrot;small, peeled & coarsely chopped**

½ **Chicken breast;cubed freshly ground black pepper**

1 tablespoon **Flour;unbleached Homemade pasta;made with**

4 **Eggs & 2/12 cups flour**

6 qt **-Water**

3 cups **Marinara sauce;(Momma's Tomato sauce) or Meat Sauce**

Ravioli Greats

Remove the roots and stems from spinach and save for later use. Rinse spinach in cold water as many times as necessary to rid it of any sand. Place in a pot with no water other than the water the spinach retains from washing. Add a pinch of salt and cook, covered for about minutes. Transfer to a colander and set aside to drain. Place oil, onion, carrot and chicken breast in a large skillet.

Add tsp salt and 1/8 tsp pepper and cook over moderate heat for 4 to 5 minutes longer or until most of the liquid has evaporated. Add flour and stir 1 more minute. Remove from heat; cool for 5 or 6 minutes, then chop very fine. Roll the dough paper thin and place over a floured board. With a feather brush dipped in cold water lightly brush the top to maintain moisture. Place mounds of spinach mixture on the dough in straight lines about 2 inches apart (measurements are from the centers of the mounds), making 8 or 9 dozen of them.

Roll out the other half of the dough paper thin and place loosely over the sheet with the mounds. With an Italian pastry wheel, press along the furrows, cutting and sealing at the same time. Bring 6 quarts of water to a boil. Add ravioli and 3 Tbsp salt. Stir until boiling resumes. Cook 4 to 5 minutes, uncovered. Drain and serve with marinara or meat sauce.

SERVES: 6-8

RAMP RAVIOLI WITH ONE-HOUR CALAMARI

4 servings
Source: Ravioli Greats

- 6 bunches **ramps, cleaned and whole**
- 1 tablespoon **black pepper**
- 2 **plum tomatoes, finely chopped**
- 1 recipe **black squid ink pasta**
- 1 cup **one-hour calamari**
- 4 tablespoons **extra virgin olive oil**
- 2 bunches **chives, in 2" sticks**

Preheat grill.

Place ramps on grill and cook until tender and smoky, about 1 minute. Remove ramps from grill and allow to cool. Chop cool ramps into 1/4-inch pieces and place in small mixing bowl with black pepper and tomatoes. Season with salt and set aside.

Bring 6 quarts water to boil and add 2 tablespoons salt.

Roll pasta to thinnest setting and cut into 3-inch squares. Place 1 tablespoon ramp mixture in center of each square and fold into a triangle. Continue until all pasta is done. Place ravioli in boiling water and simmer until cooked, about 4 to 5 minutes.

Meanwhile, heat calamari and olive oil in a 12 to 14-inch saute pan until boiling. Lower heat to simmer and add chives. Drain ravioli and toss into pan with calamari. Toss to coat and mix gently. Pour into warm platter and serve immediately.

RAVIOLI

4 servings
Source: Ravioli Greats

3 cups **flour**

1 **egg, beaten**

1 teaspoon **salt**

¾ cups **water, lukewarm**

FILLING

2 tablespoons **salad oil**

4 **green onions, chopped**

1 lb. **ground beef**

½ lb. **ground veal**

4 tablespoons **parsley, chopped**

1 cup **cooked spinach, chopped**

4 tablespoons **parmesan cheese**

2 tablespoons **bread crumbs**

Mix flour, egg, salt and lukewarm water until the dough sticks together and can be rolled out. Set aside. Heat oil in heavy skillet and brown onion.

Add the ground beef, and veal to the oil and onion. Simmer for 10 minutes. Add parsley, and spinach to the skillet and simmer for 15 minutes. Add cheese and bread crumbs, simmer for 2 minutes. Roll out the dough, cut into squares with a ravioli cutter.

Place one heaping teaspoon of filling in each square. Cover with another square. Seal by pinching together. Drop squares into 8 quarts boiling salted water and cook until tender.

RAVIOLI APPETIZERS

12 servings
Source: Ravioli Greats

1 cup **bread crumbs, soft, very fine ones**
1 teaspoon **dried oregano**
1 lb. **ravioli, cheese-filled -- cooked**
nonstick cooking spray
1 cup **spaghetti sauce, low fat OR nonfat warmed**

These tasty bites of pasta are perfect for back porch picnics, where the kitchen is close at hand. Simply prepare the ravioli ahead and pop them into the oven for 5 min when your guests arrive.

Preheat the oven to 45F. Coat 2 baking sheets with nonstick spray.

In a pie plate, combine the bread crumbs and oregano. Roll each hot ravioli in the crumb mixture until coated. Place the ravioli, 1" apart, on the baking sheets. Mist them with the nonstick spray.

Bake 1 sheet of the ravioli until lightly browned, about 5 minutes.

Bake the second sheet. Serve with the spaghetti sauce for dipping.

RAVIOLI CASSEROLE

4 servings
Source: Ravioli Greats

- 1 large **zucchini, thinly sliced**
- 1 medium **onion, thinly sliced**
- 2 teaspoons **olive oil**
- 1 jar **tomato-and-basil pasta sauce, (26-oz)**
- 1 package **frozen cheese ravioli, (24-oz) cooked**
- 1 cup **shredded mozzarella cheese, (4 oz)**
- ⅓ cup **grated parmesan cheese**

Saute zucchini and onion in hot oil in a skillet until tender. Spoon one-third of pasta sauce into a lightly greased 9-inch square baking dish.

Layer with half each of ravioli, zucchini mixture, and mozzarella; top with one-third of sauce. Repeat layers, ending with sauce. Sprinkle with Parmesan cheese.

Bake at 375°F 10 minutes or until thoroughly heated.

RAVIOLI DI ZUCCHINE E GAMBERI

6 servings
Source: Ravioli Greats

- 7 ounces **white flour**
- 4 **eggs**
- 2 ¼ lbs. **zucchini**
- 10 ounces **ricotta cheese**
- 2 ¼ lbs. **shrimp, peeled**
- 1 dash **marjoram**

Ravioli Greats

1 dash **salt**

1 dash **black pepper**

10 ounces **red ripe tomatoes, peeled and seeded**

1 pinch **parsley**

2 clove **garlic**

1 **shallots**

3 tablespoons **olive oil**

2 tablespoons **orange zest**

1 dash **marjoram**

1 dash **salt, to taste**

1 dash **black pepper, to taste**

STEP ONE: The Dough--
Make the pasta dough as per routine with the flour and eggs. The dough has to be solid but not stiff. Let it rest in the refrigerator for two hours.

STEP TWO: Prepare the Filling--
Boil the zucchini in the water with salt and the pinch of marjoram. Drain and puree them, add salt and pepper. Add the ricotta cheese.

STEP THREE: The Ravioli-
Roll the dough in very thin sheets. With the filling for the ravioli, assemble the ravioli in the size and shape of your preference.

STEP FOUR: To Prepare the Sauce--
Peel and seed the tomato; chop in small cubes. In the olive oil, cook the garlic and the shallot until they become gold-colored. Remove them from the olive oil and add the peeled shrimp and diced tomato. Cook for two minutes, add the grated orange peel, and remove from the fire.

STEP FIVE:
Cook the ravioli in salted boiling water. Add the chopped parsley to the sauce. Dress the ravioli with tomato sauce and serve.

RAVIOLI GENOVESE

4 servings
Source: Ravioli Greats

1 recipe basic fresh egg pasta (rolled to thinnest setting on machine)

=== filling ===

1 lb. **Italian sausage, without fennel seeds, cooked, crumbled, and drained**

2 cups **swiss chard, cooked, drained, and chopped**

1 cup **ricotta**

1 ½ cups **grated pecorino, divided**

3 **eggs**

½ teaspoon **freshly-grated nutmeg**

salt, to taste

freshly-ground black pepper, to taste

=== sauce ===

6 tablespoons **butter**

In a bowl, combine cooked sausage, chopped chard, ricotta, 1 cup Pecorino, eggs and nutmeg and season with salt and pepper.

Lay out 1 sheet of pasta on a work surface and dot with 1/2 tablespoons filling 2-inches apart. Lay second sheet over and press with hands to seal. Using a pizza cutter, cut out squares and set aside.

Bring 6 quarts water to a boil and add 2 tablespoons salt. Place ravioli in boiling water and cook until tender, about 4 to 5 minutes.

Melt butter in a 12-inch to 14-inch saute pan and remove from heat. Carefully drain ravioli and place in pan with butter. Toss gently over medium heat, sprinkle with remaining cheese and serve.

Ravioli Greats

RAVIOLI SOUP

4 servings
Source: Ravioli Greats

¾ lbs. **Ground beef or Italian sausage**
1 **Beef broth**
1 **Cheese ravioli or tortellini;** fresh or frozen
1 **Green beans, drained**
2 **Green onions, sliced**
1 **Tomatoes***

*Tomatoes should be Del Monte freshcut Diced Tomatoes w/ Basil, Garlic & Oregano.

In 5-qt pot, cook meat; drain. Add tomatoes, broth and 1 3/4 cups water; bring to boil. Reduce heat; stir in ravioli and cook according to pkg. directions.

Add beans and onions; heat through . Season with pepper and sprinkle with grated parmesan cheese, if desired.

RAVIOLI VEGETABLE 'LASAGNA'

6 servings
Source: Ravioli Greats

- 2 **packages chopped frozen spinach, defrosted**
- 2 tablespoons **extra-virgin olive oil**
- 4 cloves **garlic** - (to 6), finely chopped
- 2 cans **quartered artichokes in water, drained well**
- Salt, to taste
- Freshly-ground black pepper, to taste

- === WHITE SAUCE ===
- 2 tablespoons **butter**
- 2 tablespoons **all-purpose flour**
- 2 cups **vegetable or chicken stock**
- ½ cup **cream or half-and-half**
- ½ cup **grated Parmigiano-Reggiano**
- ¼ teaspoon **freshly-grated nutmeg**

Salt, to taste

Freshly-ground black pepper, to taste

=== ASSEMBLY ===

1 package **fresh ravioli** - (24 to 28 oz), such as Contadina brand, marked "Family Size"

= (or choose your favorite filling, such as wild mushroom or 4 cheese)

1 lb. **thin asparagus spears, tough ends trimmed**

2 cups **grated provolone** - (10 oz)

= (or Italian 4 Cheese Blend)

Bring a pot of water to boil for ravioli.

While water comes to a boil, drain defrosted frozen chopped spinach by wringing it dry in a kitchen towel, working over a garbage bowl or your sink. Heat a medium skillet over medium heat. Add extra-virgin olive oil, 2 tablespoons or 2 turns of the pan, and the garlic. Saute garlic in oil 1 minute, then sprinkle spinach into the garlic oil. Add artichoke heart pieces to the pan and turn to combine and heat through. Season vegetables with salt and pepper and remove from heat to a bowl.

Place skillet back on the heat and melt butter. Whisk flour into butter and cook 1 to 2 minutes. Whisk stock into flour and butter and let it bubble. Whisk in cream and Parmesan. Season sauce with nutmeg, salt and pepper and thicken 1 to 2 minutes.

Preheat broiler to high. Set rack between middle of oven groove and top rack groove, about 8 inches from heat.

When water boils, salt water, add ravioli and cook 4 to 5 minutes. Ravioli should be less than al dente, still a bit chewy -- it will continue cooking when combined with sauce and vegetables. Place a colander over ravioli as it cooks and add asparagus to it.

Cut thin, trimmed asparagus into 2-inch pieces on an angle. Steam the chopped asparagus while pasta cooks, 2 to 3 minutes, until just fork-tender, but still green. Remove asparagus and add to bowl with

42

spinach and artichokes. Place colander in your sink and drain ravioli.

Drizzle a touch of extra-virgin olive oil onto the bottom of a medium oval casserole or a rectangular baking dish and brush pan to coat evenly. Arrange a layer using 1/2 of cooked ravioli in the dish. Layer 1/2 of the cooked vegetables over the ravioli. Next, add a few ladles of sauce, then vegetables, then top casserole with the last of the ravioli. Dot top of "lasagna" with any remaining sauce and cover liberally with grated provolone or 4 cheese blend. Brown cheese 8 inches from broiler, 5 minutes.

This recipe yields 4 to 6 servings.

RAVIOLI WITH HERB-TOMATO SAUCE

5 servings
Source: Ravioli Greats

- 4 cups **torn escarole**
- ¼ cup **finely grated fresh Parmesan cheese, 1 ounce**
- 1 ½ teaspoons **minced fresh rosemary**
- ⅛ teaspoon **salt**
- ⅛ teaspoon **pepper**
- 1 clove **garlic, chopped**
- 15 ounces **canned cannellini beans, drained**
- or
- other white beans
- 40 won-ton wrappers
- Herb-Tomato Sauce
- Rosemary sprigs, optional

Place first 7 ingredients in a food processor; process until smooth, scraping sides of processor bowl occasionally. Working with 1 won ton wrapper at a time (cover remaining wrappers with a damp towel to keep them from drying out), spoon about 1 tablespoon bean mixture into center of wrapper.

Moisten edges of wrapper with water; place another wrapper over filling. Pinch 4 edges together to seal. Repeat with remaining won ton wrappers and bean mixture. Place ravioli on a baking sheet; let stand 30 minutes. Cook ravioli in boiling water 2 minutes or until tender; drain well.

NOTES : A puree of beans and escarole forms the basis for a lively filling for the ravioli. To serve, spoon Herb-Tomato Sauce over ravioli. Garnish with rosemary sprigs, if desired. Yield: 5 servings (serving size: 4 ravioli and 6 tablespoons tomato sauce).

RAVIOLI WITH BROCCOLI SAUCE

4 servings
Source: Ravioli Greats

¼ cup **olive oil**

4 **garlic cloves, chopped**

salt and pepper to taste

¼ cup **dried red pepper flakes**

1 cup **heavy cream**

1 ½ lbs. **broccoli**

¾ cups **grated parmesan cheese** *

15 ounces **frozen ricotta ravioli**

* Substitute Romano Cheese if desired.

Heat oil in medium saucepan. Add garlic, salt, pepper and red pepper. Saute until garlic is lightly browned, 5-7 mins. Add cream; cook 20 min. to thicken, stirring occasionally.

Meanwhile, cut broccoli into 1-1/2" flowerettes. Place in separate pan, cover with water and cook until tender, drain and set aside. Add cheese to sauce mixture, stir to blend. Prepare broccoli as directed, drain. Add broccoli to sauce and pour over ravioli.

RAVIOLI WITH RICOTTA FILLING

36 servings
Source: Ravioli Greats

BASIC PASTA DOUGH

4 cups **sifted flour**

½ teaspoon **salt**

4 **eggs**

6 tablespoons **very cold water**

RICOTTA FILLING

3 cups **ricotta cheese, (about**

1 ½ lbs.)

2 **eggs, well beaten**

1 tablespoon **parmesan cheese**

¾ teaspoons **salt**

¼ teaspoon **pepper**

1 ½ tablespoons **chopped parsley**

BASIC PASTA DOUGH Stir into a large bowl a mixture of: 4 c sifted flour and salt. Make a well in center of flour. Add eggs, one at a time, mixing slightly after each addition: Add gradually about: 6 Tablespoons very cold water Mix well to make a stiff dough. Turn dough onto a lightly floured surface and knead for 3 to 5 minutes until smooth and elastic. (Use shorter time if you are using a pasta machine to roll the dough.)

RICOTTA FILLING Combine in a large bowl all filling ingredients.

ASSEMBLY Divide dough into fourths. Lightly roll each portion 1/8 inch thick and cut lengthwise into 5 inch wide strips. Use the strips immediately--don't allow to dry. Place 2 teaspoons of the filling 1 1/2 inches from the narrow end and in the center of the strip. Continue along the strip, placing the filling at about 3 1/2 inch intervals.

Fold the strip in half lengthwise, covering the mounds of filling. To seal, press the edges together with the tines of a fork. Press gently between the mounds to form rectangles about 3 1/2 inches long. Cut apart with a pastry cutter and press the cut edges with the tines of a fork to seal.

COOKING In a large saucepan bring to a boil: 7 quarts water 2 Tb salt

Gradually add the ravioli (about one-half at a time). Boil rapidly, uncovered, about 20 minutes or until tender. Remove raviolis with a slotted spoon and drain. Place on a warmed platter and top with tomato sauce. Sprinkle with: grated Romano or Parmesan cheese Serve immediately.

Makes about 3 dozen ravioli.

ROSEMARY CHICKEN BREASTS, BROWN BUTTER AND BALSAMIC RAVIOLI

4 servings
Source: Ravioli Greats

=== CHICKEN ===

- 4 pieces boneless skinless chicken breast -, (6 to 8 oz ea)
- 2 tablespoons **balsamic vinegar**
- = (just enough to coat chicken lightly)
- 2 tablespoons **extra-virgin olive oil**
- 3 sprigs **rosemary, leaves stripped,**
- and chopped - (abt 2 tbspns)
- Salt, to taste
- Coarsely-ground black pepper, to taste
- 4 cloves **garlic, smashed**

=== RAVIOLI ===

- 1 package **fresh any-flavor-filling ravioli** -, (12 to 16 oz)
- 3 tablespoons **butter, cut small pieces**
- 2 tablespoons **balsamic vinegar**
- 2 handfuls grated **Parmigiano-Reggiano**
- Salt, to taste
- Freshly-ground black pepper, to taste
- ¼ cup **chopped flat-leaf parsley**
- **Warm Spinach Salad with Pancetta**, (see recipe)

Coat chicken in balsamic vinegar, then olive oil. Season chicken with rosemary, salt and pepper and let stand 10 minutes.

Bring a large pot of water to a boil for ravioli. Salt water and drop ravioli in water. Cook 8 minutes or until raviolis expand, float to top of water, and are al dente.

Heat a medium nonstick skillet over medium-high heat. Add chicken breasts and cracked garlic to the pan. Cook chicken 12 minutes, or until juices run clear, turning occasionally. The balsamic vinegar will produce a deep brown, sweet finish on the chicken as it cooks.

When the chicken is 2 or 3 minutes away from done, heat a second skillet over medium-low to medium heat. To the second skillet, add butter to the pan and let it begin to brown.

Remove chicken from the first skillet and transfer to a warm platter.

When the butter for the ravioli has browned, add cooked ravioli to the pan and turn in butter to heat through. Add balsamic vinegar to the ravioli and cook a minute or 2 longer to reduce the vinegar and glaze the ravioli. The vinegar will become thick and syrup like. Add cheese, parsley, salt and pepper to the pasta and remove the pan from the heat.

Serve chicken along side ravioli and Warm Spinach Salad With Pancetta And Sweet Vinaigrette, all on the same dinner plate.

This recipe yields 4 servings.

SOUTHWESTERN WON TON RAVIOLI

1 servings
Source: Ravioli Greats

All-purpose flour

40 won ton skins, (8 oz.)

Chili-cheese filling or

chorizo-tomatillo filling, see recipes

Chipotle-cream sauce or lime sauce, see recipes

1. In a small bowl, blend 1 1/2 teaspoons flour with 1 1/2 tablespoons water.

2. On a lightly floured board, lay 4 to 6 won ton skins flat. Spoon 1 tablespoon filling onto center of each. Brush edges of skins with flour-water mixture. Align another won ton skin over each one on the board; firmly press edges together to seal. If desired, trim edges slightly with a zigzag ravioli cutter.

3. Lay filled ravioli, side by side but not touching, on a flour-dusted baking sheet. Cover with plastic wrap to prevent drying. Repeat to fill remaining ravioli, using additional pans as required.

4. In a 5- to 6-quart pan, bring 3 quarts water to a boil over high heat. Add half the ravioli at a time; cook until wrappers are just tender to bite, 2 to 3 minutes.

5. As ravioli cook, spoon hot chipotle sauce equally onto heated plates (or spoon half the lime sauce onto plates).

6. With a slotted spoon, lift 1 ravioli at a time from water, drain and lay on plates. If using lime sauce, spoon remainder equally over ravioli.

NOTES: Serve chili-cheese-filled ravioli with chipotle-cream sauce. Serve chorizo-tomatillo-filled ravioli with lime sauce. If making ravioli ahead, complete through step 2, cover, and chill up to 1 day. Or freeze in a single layer until firm, transfer to an airtight container, and freeze up to 1 month; cook frozen, allowing 6 to 8 minutes.

MAKES: About 20 pieces; 4 servings

Chili-Cheese Filling
In a food processor, whirl 1 can (4 oz.) diced green chilies, 2 tablespoons chopped onion, 1 1/2 teaspoons chopped garlic, 1 1/2 cups (6 oz.) grated cotija or parmesan cheese, and 1 large egg until smooth. Or mince vegetables, place in a bowl, and mix with cheese

and egg.

Lime Sauce
In a bowl, mix 1/3 cup extra-virgin olive oil, 3 tablespoons lime juice, and 1 1/2 tablespoons grated parmesan cheese. Add salt and cracked pepper to taste.

SPICY VEGETABLE VINAIGRETTE

4 servings
Source: Ravioli Greats

- 3 tablespoons **water**
- 2 tablespoons **extra-virgin olive oil**
- ⅓ cup **balsamic vinegar**
- 2 tablespoons **finely chopped onion**
- 2 tablespoons **finely chopped green onions**
- 2 tablespoons **finely chopped squash**
- 2 tablespoons **finely chopped zucchini**
- 2 tablespoons **finely chopped fresh parsley**
- ¼ teaspoon **salt**
- ¼ teaspoon **crushed red pepper**
- ⅛ teaspoon **black pepper**

Combine all ingredients in a small bowl; stir well. Let stand at room temperature at least 1 hour. Yield: 1 cup (serving size: 1/4 cup).

ST. LOUIS TOASTED RAVIOLI

14 servings
Source: Ravioli Greats

- 1 lb. **frozen ravioli**
- 2 tablespoons **milk**
- 1 **egg**
- ⅔ cups **fine, dry seasoned bread crumbs**
- **up to 1 cup**

shortening or oil, for deep

1 cup **spaghetti sauce, or pizza sauce**

grated parmesan cheese

Thaw the ravioli. In a mixing bowl, beat together the milk and egg. Dip each ravioli into the mixture; coat with crumbs. In a heavy 3-quart saucepan, heat 2 inches of oil to 350°F.

Fry the ravioli, a few at a time, in hot oil for 1 minute per side, or until golden. Drain on paper towels; keep warm in a 300°F oven while frying the rest.

Heat the sauce. Sprinkle the ravioli with Parmesan. Serve with warm sauce for dipping.

Makes 12 to 14 appetizers.

SUMMER VEGETABLE RAVIOLI WITH SPICY VINAIGRETTE

4 servings
Source: Ravioli Greats

Spicy Vegetable Vinaigrette

1 teaspoon **olive oil**

⅓ cup **diced peeled eggplant**

⅓ cup **diced squash**

⅓ cup **diced zucchini**

¼ cup **finely chopped onion**

2 tablespoons **finely chopped celery**

2 tablespoons **finely chopped green bell pepper**

2 tablespoons **finely chopped green onions**

3 cloves **garlic, minced**

½ cup **seeded chopped unpeeled tomato**

2 tablespoons **chopped fresh parsley**

16 **wonton wrappers**, (3-1/4 x 3-inch)

1 **egg white,** lightly beaten

¼ cup **grated fresh Parmesan cheese**

SPICY VEGETABLE VINAIGRETTE:

Ravioli Greats

- 3 tablespoons **water**
- 2 tablespoons **extra-virgin olive oil**
- ⅓ cup **balsamic vinegar**
- 2 tablespoons **finely chopped onion**
- 2 tablespoons **finely chopped green onions**
- 2 tablespoons **finely chopped squash**
- 2 tablespoons **finely chopped zucchini**
- 2 tablespoons **finely chopped fresh parsley**
- ¼ teaspoon **salt**
- ¼ teaspoon **crushed red pepper**
- ⅛ teaspoon **black pepper**

Prepare Spicy Vegetable Vinaigrette, and set aside.

Heat oil in a nonstick skillet over high heat. Add eggplant and next 7 ingredients; sauté 2 minutes. Combine eggplant mixture, tomato, and parsley in a bowl; stir well, and set aside.

To make ravioli, work with 1 wonton wrapper at a time (cover remaining wrappers with a damp towel to keep them from drying out), and brush 8 wrappers with egg white. Spoon about 2 tablespoons vegetable mixture into center of each wrapper, and top each with another wrapper, stretching top wrapper slightly to meet edges of bottom wrapper. Press edges together with a fork to seal.

Fill a large Dutch oven with water, and bring to a boil over medium-high heat. Add 4 ravioli (cover the remaining ravioli with a damp towel to keep them from drying out), and cook 5 minutes, turning them carefully in the water halfway through cooking time.

Remove ravioli with a slotted spoon, and set aside; repeat procedure with remaining ravioli. Place 2 ravioli in each of 4 shallow bowls, and top with 1/4 cup Spicy Vegetable Vinaigrette. Yield: 4 appetizers.

SPICY VEGETABLE VINAIGRETTE:

Combine all ingredients in a small bowl: stir well. Let stand at room temperature at least 1 hour. Yield: 1 cup (serving size: 1/4 cup).

Serving Ideas : Sprinkle each serving with 1 tablespoon Parmesan cheese.

SWEET PEPPER RAVIOLI (ADAPTED FROM WILLIAM-SONOMA PASTA)

1 servings
Source: Ravioli Greats

3 cups **all-purpose flour, or more**

3 **large eggs, at room temperature**

½ lb. **red peppers, roasted and peeled, julienned**

½ teaspoon **salt**

1 **ricotta cheese, (we used low fat)**

2 **eggs**

1 tablespoon **chopped parsley**

½ cup **parmesan cheese, grated**

salt and pepper, to taste

(Their recipe calls for you to place the flour, 3 eggs, peppers and salt in a food processor and pulse until mixture forms a uniform-colored ball) Old-fashioned method (or poor college student method) Puree the pepper in a blender.

Make a mound of the flour with a well in the center, add the salt. Put the pepper and the eggs into the well and blend with a fork until that becomes too difficult, then knead on a floured surface until smooth and elastic and not too soft. If it's too dry, add liquid, too sticky, add flour.

In a bowl, beat ricotta cheese, add eggs (2), parsley, cheese, salt and pepper and beat until blended.

Roll out the pasta dough according to instructions for ravioli rack (we did it three times through a hand-cranked pasta machine) and fill with cheese (1 tsp, maybe less).

To cook: boil in lightly salted water for about 3 minutes or until tender. We served it with a standard pasta sauce (crushed tomatoes, paste, onions, peppers, lots o' garlic, mustard powder, herbs.

SWORDFISH RAVIOLI WITH OLIVE PESTO

4 servings
Source: Ravioli Greats

½ lb. **cooked swordfish (from involtini or paillard recipe)**

½ cup **basic tomato sauce**

4 **scallions, thinly sliced, plus**

2 **scallions, thinly sliced**

10 **basil leaves, chiffonade**

½ **recipe basic pasta**

4 tablespoons **extra virgin olive oil**

2 tablespoons **butter**

2 tablespoons **black olive paste**

Bring 6 quarts water to boil and add 2 tablespoons salt.

Roughly chop swordfish and place in mixing bowl. Add tomato sauce, scallions and basil and stir well to combine. Roll pasta out to thinnest setting on pasta machine and cut out eight 5 by 5 squares. Divide swordfish mixture among four squares and place the remaining four squares on each one. Carefully press the edges of the pasta together to form large square packages of ravioli. Place ravioli in boiling water and lower heat to high simmer and cook for four to five minutes, or until pasta is tender and filling is hot.

Meanwhile, place olive oil and butter in a 12 to 14-inch saute pan over medium heat. Cook until butter is bubbling and add black olive paste. Let pan sit off heat until ravioli are done. Carefully remove ravioli with a large slotted spoon and gently place all four in pan with olive paste mixture. Put pan over medium heat. Gently shake pan to cover ravioli, and scallions and serve immediately.

Chapter 2: N-Z

TOASTED RAVIOLI

12 servings
Source: Ravioli Greats

2 tablespoons **milk**

1 large **egg, lightly beaten**

¾ cups **dry Italian-seasoned breadcrumbs**

½ **package frozen cheese-filled ravioli, thawed**

vegetable oil

parmesan cheese, grated

pizza sauce

Combine milk and egg. Place breadcrumbs in shallow bowl. Dip ravioli in milk mixture and coat with breadcrumbs. Pour oil to depth of 2 inches in Dutch oven. Heat to 350°F.

Fry ravioli, a few at a time, 1 minute on each side or until golden. Drain on paper towels. Sprinkle with Parmesan cheese.

Serve immediately with warm pizza sauce.

TURKEY CUTLETS WITH FRIED RAVIOLI

4 servings
Source: Ravioli Greats

1 package **fresh ravioli** - (12 to 14 oz)

= (filled with cheese, spinach or mushroom and cheese)

Salt, as needed

1 cup **cornmeal**

¼ cup **grated Parmigiano-Reggiano or Romano**

½ teaspoon **freshly-grated or ground nutmeg**

½ teaspoon **freshly-ground black pepper**

3 tablespoons **extra-virgin olive oil**

Ravioli Greats

- 2 tablespoons **butter**
- 1 ⅓ lbs. **turkey cutlets**
- 2 tablespoons **fresh rosemary leaves, chopped**
- = (the yield of a few sprigs, stripped)
- **Coarsely-ground black pepper, to taste**
- **Fresh bay leaves, 1 for each cutlet**
- = (or small dried bay leaves)
- 2 **lemons, zested and juiced**
- 1 cup **dry white wine or dry vermouth**
- **Rapini With Golden Raisins,** (see recipe)

Place a large pot of water to boil over high heat. Add a healthy dose of salt to boiling water to season it. Add ravioli and cook to package directions for al dente.

Pour cornmeal onto a plate and combine with grated cheese, then season with nutmeg and black pepper. Heat a medium nonstick skillet over moderate heat and add 1 tablespoon oil and 1 tablespoon butter. Drain ravioli. Dust hot, cooked ravioli with cornmeal. Add coated ravioli to the skillet and brown on both sides, 3 or 4 minutes total.

While pasta is working, preheat a large skillet for cutlets over medium to medium-high heat. Season turkey cutlets with chopped rosemary, salt and pepper. Choose small fresh or dried bay leaves or halve large leaves with kitchen scissors. Press a small bay leaf or 1/2 leaf into each turkey cutlet.

Add 2 tablespoons extra-virgin olive oil to the pan; 2 turns around the pan in a slow stream. Turn cutlets over as you set them into the pan so that the bay leaf faces down. Cook the cutlets in a single layer, working in 2 batches if necessary. Saute the cutlets 4 or 5 minutes on each side. Transfer to a warm plate.

Add the lemon zest and juice to the pan and deglaze the pan with wine or vermouth, pulling up any pan drippings with a whisk. Add remaining tablespoon butter to the pan, whisk it in and pour the pan sauce down over the cutlets. Serve the cutlets along side the fried ravioli with Rapini With Golden Raisins or a green tossed salad.

Chapter 2: N–Z

This recipe yields 4 servings.

VEGETABLE FILLED RAVIOLI

30 servings
Source: Ravioli Greats

--**pasta dough**---

4 cups **durham flour**

16 **egg yolks**

¼ teaspoon **kosher salt**

2 teaspoons **olive oil**

5 tablespoons **water**

--**vegetable filling**---

1 **yellow pepper, diced small**

1 **red bell pepper, diced small**

1 **zucchini, diced small**

½ **fennel bulb, diced small**

1 **carrot peeled, diced small**

4 **green onions, diced small**

4 tablespoons **olive oil**

2 **cloves garlic**

⅛ teaspoon **black pepper**

1 tablespoon **kosher salt**

1 **whole egg**

1 teaspoon **fresh basil, chopped**

1 teaspoon **fresh flat leaf parsely, chopped**

4 tablespoons **parmesan cheese, grated -pasta sauce---**

4 tablespoons **olive oil**

1 tablespoon **chopped garlic**

3 **cleaned artichokes, thinly sliced**

1 pint **cherry tomatoes, halved**

4 ounces **white wine**

2 cups **vegetable or chicken stock**

1 teaspoon **chopped parsely**

salt and pepper to taste

Ravioli dough: Place flour in a mixing bowl and make a well. Add egg yolks, salt, olive oil and water. Mix with a fork, then with hands until a small dough has been formed. Refrigerate for 1/2 hour before using the dough.

Filling: Mix all diced vegetables in a bowl. Saute garlic in olive oil for 2 minutes then add small diced vegetables and cook for five minutes or until vegetables turn soft. Add saute to vegetables. Let filling cool.

Making the ravioli: Roll pasta dough with a rolling pin until dough is almost transparent. With a pizza cutter, cut 3 inch squares from the dough. Place 1 tablespoon of filling in one square. Brush the sides of the square with water then place another square on top. Make sure to seal sides with fingers.

Sauce: Saute artichokes and garlic in olive oil for five minutes. Add white wine and cook for 2 minutes. Add chicken stock or vegetable stock and cherry tomatoes. Season with salt and pepper.

Finishing the meal: Bring 4 gallons of water to boil with kosher salt. Cook ravioli for 4 minutes then add to sauce. Cook ravioli with sauce for one more minute, add arugula and serve. Garnish with chopped parsely. Serve with parmesan cheese.

WHITE BEAN RAVIOLI WITH BALSAMIC VINEGAR BROWN BUTTER

4 servings
Source: Ravioli Greats

2 cups **cooked white beans, divided**

½ cup **virgin olive oil**

1 **egg**

½ cup **balsamic vinegar, divided**

½ cup **freshly-ground parmesan cheese**

¼ cup **finely-chopped Italian parsley**

salt, to taste

freshly-ground black pepper, to taste

1 recipe roasted beet pasta, see * note

(rolled out on thinnest setting to 4 sheet

6 ounces **sweet butter**

=== garnish ===

4 tablespoons **freshly-ground parmesan cheese**	2 tablespoons **finely-chopped Italian parsley**

Filling: In a food processor, blend one cup cooked white beans with virgin olive oil, 1/4 cup balsamic vinegar, grated Parmesan cheese, egg and parsley until smooth (about 1 minute). Remove to medium mixing bowl and stir in remaining cup of beans. Season to taste with salt and pepper.

Assembly: Lay out 1 sheet of pasta and cut into 8 pieces, 3 1/2-inches by 3 1/2-inches. Place 1 1/2 tablespoons filling in center of each square and fold corner to corner to form triangle shaped pillow. Press edge firmly around to seal. Continue with all remaining pasta. Should yield 32 ravioli. These can be set aside on a baking tray in refrigerator for 6 hours, separated by a kitchen towel.

To cook: Bring 6 quarts water to boil in a large spaghetti pot and add 2 tablespoons salt. Drop ravioli into water and return to boil. Lower heat slightly and cook just below boiling for 3 minutes.

Meanwhile, place sweet butter in 10-inch to 12-inch saute pan and cook until foam subsides and butter begins to brown. Turn off heat and add remaining 1/4 cup balsamic vinegar (careful; it will spatter). Remove ravioli from cooking liquid with spider and place in pan with butter and vinegar. Toss over medium heat and sprinkle with remaining cheese and parsley. Divide among 4 plates and serve immediately.

WHITE CHOCOLATE RAVIOLI

8 servings
Source: Ravioli Greats

3 ounces **white chocolate bars, (Tobler) halved crosswise**	½ cup **hazelnuts, toasted and husked – coarsely chopped**

Ravioli Greats

8 mint sprigs	1 pn salt
*** **mousse** ***	1 pn **cream of tartar**
8 ounces **chocolate –extra bittersweet**	4 tablespoons **sugar**
or semisweet, chopped	¾ cups **whipping cream – well chilled**
¼ cup **butter – unsalted**	1 teaspoon **vanilla**
2 **eggs, separated** – at room temperature	

MOUSSE: Melt the chocolate and butter in top of a double boiler over barely simmering water. Stir until smooth. Transfer to medium bowl. Whisk in egg yolks. Beat egg whites, salt and cream of tartar in another bowl until soft peaks form. Add 2 tablespoons sugar and beat until stiff but not dry. Fold in chocolate.

In another bowl, beat cream with 2 tablespoons of sugar and vanilla until slightly thickened. Fold into chocolate. Pour into metal bowl. Cover and chill over night.

Chill ravioli mold in freezer. Preheat oven on lowest setting for 5 minutes. Turn off oven. Place white chocolate on baking sheets. Place in turned off oven and let stand until soft enough to yield when pressed with finger, about 5 minutes.

Roll one piece of chocolate out on a sheet of parchment paper to flatten slightly. Lift chocolate off paper, using a thin knife if necessary. Turn pasta machine to widest setting. Run chocolate through. Adjust pasta machine to next narrower setting. Run chocolate through the machine again.

Repeat, narrowing rollers after each run until chocolate is 1/16 inch thick. Quickly press chocolate into chilled ravioli mold.

Fill each ravioli with 1 to 1 1/2 tablespoons of mousse filling. Repeat rolling with second piece of chocolate, resoftening in oven as necessary. Complete ravioli. Seal with rolling pin. Invert mold, pressing gently to release ravioli. Cut into separate pieces with ravioli cutter or knife if necessary. Place on chilled baking sheet and refrigerate.

Before serving, let chocolate ravioli stand at room temperature for 30 minutes. Arrange four ravioli on each plate. Sprinkle with nuts and garnish with mint.

WHITE MEAT RAVIOLI

4 servings
Source: Ravioli Greats

¾ lbs. **chicken breast or veal or canned tuna, chopped** ground

2 tablespoons **shallots, finely chopped**

2 **plum tomatoes, chopped**

1 teaspoon **dried leaf sage, crumbled**

¼ teaspoon **mace**

¼ cup **parmeson or romano cheese** grated

½ cup **parsley, chopped**

½ teaspoon **black pepper, coursely** ground

1 tablespoon **brandy or dry sherry**

pasta dough

SAUCE

2 tablespoons **olive oil**

4 **scallions, thinly sliced**

2 cloves **garlic, minced**

1 cup **tomatoes, crushed**

1 cup **tomato sauce**

1 tablespoon **basil**

Place all ingredients, except pasta, in a large mixing bowl and combine thoroughly. Fill ravioli with mixture.

Heat oil over medium heat. Stir-fry scallions and garlic for about 30 seconds. Add tomatoes, tomato sauce and basil. Stir. Simmer for 10-15 minutes.

WILD MUSHROOM RAVIOLI WITH EGGPLANT AND GOAT CHEESE

4 servings
Source: Ravioli Greats

- 1 ¼ lbs. **eggplant**
- = (four 5" to 6" **Japanese eggplants** or
- a **small, firm eggplant**)
- 2 tablespoons **extra-virgin olive oil**
- 3 cloves **garlic, chopped**
- **Salt,** to taste
- **Freshly-ground black pepper,** to taste
- 1 package **fresh wild mushroom ravioli** - (12 oz)
- 2 medium **vine ripe tomatoes** - (abt 8 oz)
- 8 ounces **goat cheese,** to crumble
- 20 **fresh basil leaves, torn or shredded**

Place a pot of water on the stove to boil for pasta.

Trim half of the skin from the eggplant. Leaving a little skin on will add color and texture to the dish. The small, firm eggplants are not too bitter and when they are firm, they will not soak up as much oil, so they do not need to be salted and pressed. However, if you leave all the skin, especially when you use baby eggplant, the skin overpowers the flavor of the flesh and the texture is too tough overall.

Heat a medium nonstick skillet over medium-high heat. Cut the eggplant into 1-inch by 1/2-inch bite-size pieces. Add 2 turns of extra-virgin olive oil to the pan, the garlic and the eggplant. Turn and toss the eggplant and season it with salt and pepper. Let it brown lightly at edges, about 5 minutes, then reduce heat to medium low and continue to cook.

Add salt and ravioli to the pasta water and simmer to package directions, about 5 or 6 minutes, until just tender.

While the pasta cooks, dice tomatoes and add them to the cooking eggplant. Adjust seasoning with salt and pepper.

Drain cooked pasta and plate individually or on a platter. Top with eggplant and tomatoes and all of the basil and cheese. If you plate individually, use 1/4 of the basil and 2 ounces of cheese, crumbled, per portion.

This recipe yields 4 servings.

WONTON SKIN RAVIOLIS

4 servings
Source: Ravioli Greats

50 wonton wrappers -, (about 1 1/2 pkgs)
1 egg, beaten with
1 teaspoon **water, for egg wash**
1 recipe ravioli filling,
see * note

Lay out 8 wonton wrappers on counter in front of you. Paint each one lightly with beaten egg. Place 1 tablespoon filling in the center of each ravioli. Seal by placing 8 additional wonton wrappers on top to cover each square. Pick up each ravioli and press well all around edges to seal. For a good seal, make sure no filling is stuck in the edges.

Square ravioli can be left as is or cut into festive shapes (stars, hearts, etc.) with a medium cookie cutter. Place the ravioli upside down on a cookie sheet lined with parchment. Lay out 8 more wrappers and repeat the process until either wrappers or filling is gone. Lay additional parchment or plastic wrap between layers of ravioli as needed as you lay them on the cookie sheet. The entire cookie sheet can be wrapped well and refrigerated for 12 days.

When ready to cook ravioli, bring large pot of salted water to a boil.

Lower heat to a simmer, give the water a good stir to form a whirlpool effect and quickly drop in 12 to 15 raviolis one by one, stirring gently to separate them as they hit the water. Poach gently 2 to 3 minutes, or until ravioli puff up, float to the surface and are opaque in the center (in the case of raw poultry or fish fillings).

Remove ravioli from pot with a slotted spoon and reserve.

Cook remaining ravioli in same manner.

Serve with sauce, butter, or oil, or in broth, and with or without cheese.

This recipe yields 25 ravioli; 4 main-course or 6 appetizer servings.

Comments: Every culture has its version of the dumpling, or tasty tidbit wrapped up in dough. Think about empanadas, calzone, ravioli, pierogi, or dim sum, and you'll see that every culture has taken its best flavors and put them inside some dough! Here we fill Chinese wonton wrappers, a form of pasta with an interesting slippery texture due to some cornstarch in the dough, with some flavors kids love.

These ravioli are easy and fun to make with kids. Little ones enjoy brushing on the glue (egg wash) while older kids love to help seal and cut out the dumplings. Be sure kids don't handle or taste raw poultry, meat or fish.

Index

○ ○ ○ ○ ○

Index

, 21
(4 oz), 38
(about 2 cups), 1
(from involtini or paillard, 53
(rolled out on thinnest, 57
(rolled to thinnest setting, 40
(tobler) halved crosswise, 58
), 45
*** mousse ***, 59
basic pasta dough, 45
creamy cheese sauce, 21
dough, 29
filling, 11, 29, 36
for garnish, 33
for ravioli, 33
garnish, 9
pasta, 11
ricotta filling, 45
sauce, 12, 30, 60
to cook, 30
*if using self-rising, 8, 27
--filling---, 24
--meat mixture---, 22
--pasta dough---, 56
--vegetable filling---, 56
-water, 34
/ " wonton wrappers, 11
300 millilit cream, 22
8 oz contain soft-style, 10
8.5x11" fresh pasta sheets, 16
= (filled with cheese, 54
= (four 5" to 6" japanese eggplants or, 61
= (just enough to coat chicken lightly), 46
= (or choose your favorite filling, 42
= (or italian 4 cheese blend), 42
= (or small dried bay leaves), 55
= (the yield of a few sprigs, 55
=== assembly ===, 13, 42
=== caramelized walnuts ===, 13
=== chicken ===, 46
=== filling ===, 13, 28, 40
=== garnish ===, 57
=== ravioli ===, 46
=== sauce ===, 28, 40
=== white sauce ===, 41
a small, 61
all-purpose flour, 41, 47, 52
all-purpose flour*, 8, 27
almonds, 27
american cheese, 18
anchovy fillets, 21
and chopped - (abt 2 tbspns), 46
and diced, 13, 13
and onion, 10
artichoke hearts, 24
arugula leaves, 24, 24
as wild mushroom or 4 cheese), 42
asparagus, 1
baked until soft,, 28
baking apple, 13
baking soda, 8, 27
baking soda and salt., 27
baking soda and salt. rease, 8
balsamic vinegar, 46, 46, 49, 51, 57

64

basic tomato sauce, 53
basil, 60
basil leaves, 53
basil; fresh, 11
beef broth, 41
beef ground, 23
beurre blanc, 20
black olive paste, 53
black pepper, 16, 35, 49, 51, 56, 60
blueberry syrup, 13
boiling water, 16
brand, 42
brandy or dry sherry, 60
bread crumbs, 36, 37
bread crumbs soft, 23
bread crumbs-soft, 19
breadcrumbs, 15, 54
broccoli, 44
brown sugar - (lightly packed), 13
bunches chives, 35
bunches ramps, 35
butter, 1, 2, 13, 13, 21, 40, 41, 46, 53, 55
butter - unsalted, 59
butterfly macaroni, 23
can tomato paste, 22
can tomato sauce, 23
canned cannellini beans, 43
canned it, 12
canned tuna, 60
cans quartered artichokes in water, 41
carrot peeled, 56
carrot;small,, 34
celery - (15 oz), 6
cheddar cheese-shredded, 19
cheese, 28, 33
cheese ravioli, 1
cheese ravioli or tortellini;, 41
cherry tomatoes, 56
chicken breast or veal or, 60
chicken breast tenders - (3/4 to 1 lb), 6
chicken breast;cubed freshly, 34

chicken broth, 6
chicken filling, 7
chili-cheese filling or, 47
chipotle-cream sauce or lime sauce, 47
chocolate -extra bittersweet, 59
chopped, 29, 56
chopped artichoke hearts,, 24
chopped flat-leaf parsley, 46
chopped fresh herbs, 5, 24
chopped fresh parsley, 21, 50
chopped frozen spinach, 6
chopped garlic, 56
chopped parsley, 56
chopped parsley, 45, 52
chopped sage leaves, 33
chorizo-tomatillo filling, 47
cinnamon, 13
cinnamon stick, 13
cleaned artichokes, 56
clove garlic, 4
cloves garlic, 16, 18, 56, 60
coarsely grated parmesan, 33
coarsely-ground black pepper, 46, 55
confit of duck leg, 9
cooked, 37
cooked chicken, 7
cooked spinach, 7, 36
cooked swordfish, 53
cooked white beans, 57
cooking oil, 11
cornmeal, 54
craig gardiner, 3
cream, 2, 21
cream cheese with chives, 10
cream or half-and-half, 41
crushed red pepper, 49, 51
crusty italian bread or rolls, 6
cube, 22
cups., 8, 27
dash black pepper, 39, 39
dash marjoram, 38, 39
dash salt, 39, 39

Index

diced carrot, 4
diced celery, 4
diced peeled eggplant, 50
diced shallots, 5
diced spanish onion, 4
diced squash, 50
diced zucchini, 50
dijon mustard, 1
dried, 11
dried leaf sage, 60
dried oregano, 16, 37
dried oregano leaves, 15
dried parsley, 18
dried red pepper flakes, 44
dried tomatoes, 4
dry italian-seasoned, 54
dry white wine or dry vermouth, 55
durham flour, 56
egg, 7, 15, 36, 49, 57, 62
egg white, 50
egg yolks, 56
eggplant, 61
eggs, 7, 8, 12, 18, 23, 27, 32, 38, 40, 45, 45, 52, 59
eggs & 2/12 cups flour, 34
eggs-well beaten, 19
extra virgin olive oil, 35, 53
extra-virgin olive oil, 6, 28, 41, 46, 49, 51, 54, 61
fennel bulb, 56
fine, 49
fine dry bread crumbs, 15
fine ones, 37
finely chopped celery, 50
finely chopped fresh parsley, 49, 51
finely chopped green bell pepper, 50
finely chopped green onions, 49, 50, 51
finely chopped onion, 49, 50, 51
finely chopped squash, 49, 51
finely chopped walnuts, 8
finely chopped zucchini, 49, 51

finely grated fresh parmesan cheese, 43
finely shredded lemon peel, 27
finely-chopped, 57, 58
flat leafed parsley, 9
flat leafed parsley leaves, 9
flat-leaf parsley leaves, 5
flour, 8, 12, 29, 36
flour - omit, 27
flour to, 8, 27
flour;unbleached, 34
four-ounce lamb paillardes (5"x5"x1/8"), 20
fresh any-flavor-filling ravioli -, 46
fresh basil, 1, 3, 16, 56
fresh basil leaves, 16, 61
fresh bay leaves, 55
fresh flat leaf parsley,, 56
fresh flat-leaf parsley,, 24
fresh italian parsley, 20
fresh or frozen, 41
fresh parmesan cheese, 21
fresh parsley, 16
fresh ravioli, 6
fresh ravioli - (12 to 14 oz), 54
fresh ravioli - (24 to 28 oz), 42
fresh rosemary leaves, 55
fresh savory, 20
fresh thyme, 4
fresh wild mushroom ravioli - (12 oz), 61
freshly chopped sage, 33
freshly ground nutmeg, 24
freshly ground pepper, 11
freshly-grated nutmeg, 40, 41
freshly-grated or ground nutmeg, 54
freshly-ground, 57, 58
freshly-ground black pepper, 6, 41, 42, 46, 54, 61
freshly-ground black pepper,, 28, 40, 57
frozen ravioli, 49
frozen ricotta ravioli, 44

garlic, 3, 6, 11, 15, 19, 20, 39, 43, 46, 50, 61
garlic - (to 6), 41
garlic clove, 9
garlic cloves, 44
garlic salt, 23
garnish, 1
ginger, 30
goat cheese, 4, 20, 61
good quality chicken stock, 33
grated, 60
grated fresh parmesan cheese, 21, 22, 50
grated lemon rind, 21
grated parmesan, 7
grated parmesan cheese, 1, 24, 33, 38, 50
grated parmesan cheese *, 44
grated parmigiano-reggiano, 41
grated parmigiano-reggiano or romano, 6, 54
grated pecorino, 40
grated pecorino-romano, 28
grated pepper finely, 1
grated provolone - (10 oz), 42
green beans, 41
green onion, 30
green onions, 36, 41, 56
ground, 60
ground allspice, 13
ground beef, 17, 19, 36
ground beef or italian, 41
ground black pepper, 34
ground nutmeg, 21
ground raw chicken or turkey, 10
ground sage, 23
ground veal, 36
handfuls grated parmigiano-reggiano, 46
hazelnuts, 15, 58
head broccoli florets, 3
heavy cream, 44
herb-tomato sauce, 43

homemade pasta;made with, 34
honey, 8, 27, 27
hot chili oil, 30
hot cooked pasta, 4
italian bread crumbs, 16
italian parsley, 57, 58
italian sausage, 40
jar spaghetti sauce, 17
jar tomato-and-basil, 38
kosher salt, 56, 56
large carrots, 4
large celery roots, 4
large egg, 54
large egg -, 28
large eggs, 52
large garlic clove, 22
large garlic cloves,, 1
large portobello mushrooms, 4
large red bell pepper,, 1
large russet potatoes,, 28
large tomatoes, 16
large zucchini, 38
lean ground beef, 18
leaves bulk salt, 34
lemon juice, 3, 21, 27
lemon peel, 12
lemons, 55
longhorn cheese, 18
macaroni-cooked, 19
mace, 60
madeira, 12
margarine or butter, 8, 27
marinara sauce or spaghetti, 11
marinara sauce;(momma's, 34
mascarpone cheese, 24
mastoccioli pasta, 18
meat -or- cheese filled, 15
medium eggplant, 11
medium onion, 18, 38
medium onion-chopped, 19
medium onions, 22
medium shells, 18

Index

medium vine ripe tomatoes – (abt 8 oz), 61
milk, 1, 27, 49, 54
minced, 24
minced chicken, 21
minced fresh basil, 12
minced fresh rosemary, 43
minced garlic, 24
minced parsley, 7
miniature chocolate chips, 8
mint sprigs, 59
mozzarella cheese, 18
mushroom and cheese), 54
mushrooms, 1
nonstick cooking spray, 37
nutmeg, 16, 32
oil, 18, 19, 19
olive oil, 3, 3, 4, 4, 11, 15, 20, 21, 34, 38, 39, 44, 50, 56, 56, 56, 60
olive or vegetable oil, 32
on machine), 40
one-hour calamari, 35
onion;small, 34
onions, 15
optional **, 9
or, 43
or drained chopped, 12
or fresh parmesan, 4
or nonfat, 37
or semisweet, 59
orange zest, 39
oregano, 18, 23
other white beans, 43
package, 19
package frozen cheese, 38
package frozen cheese-filled, 54
package frozen chopped, 18
packages chopped frozen spinach, 41
packages spinach, 23
paprika, 1
parmesan cheese, 3, 3, 15, 18, 23, 36, 45, 52, 54, 56, 57, 58
parmeson or romano cheese, 60
parsley, 36, 60
parsley; chopped, 23
parsley; fresh, 11
pasta, 24, 40
pasta dough, 60
pasta sauce, 38
pears, 13
peeled & coarsely chopped, 34
peeled and mashed, 28
peeled and minced, 1
pepper, 19, 43, 45
perfect fresh sage leaves, 28
pieces boneless skinless chicken breast –, 46
pieces string, 20
pinch cayenne pepper, 2
pinch fresh ground black pepper, 20, 20
pinch parsley, 39
pinch salt, 2, 20
pinch white pepper, 2
pine nuts, 20
pink peppercorns, 20
pinot noir, 13
pizza sauce, 54
plain flour, 22
plum tomatoes, 35, 60
pn cream of tartar, 59
pn grated nutmeg, 28
pn salt, 59
pn white pepper, 30
poached tomato base, 16
poppy seed, 27, 27
pork, 29
pre-sliced fresh mushrooms, 6
pumpkin, 32
pumpkin seed sauce, 32
quantity plain pasta dough, 21
rapini with golden raisins, 55
ravioli, 3, 37, 38, 54
ravioli; frozen, 15
rease, 27
recipe basic fresh egg, 40

Ravioli Greats

recipe basic pasta, 53
recipe black squid ink pasta, 35
recipe follows, 5
recipe green pasta, 28
recipe ravioli filling,, 62
recipe red wine reduction,, 5
recipe roasted beet pasta,, 57
recipe), 53
red bell pepper, 56
red peppers, 52
red rice vinegar, 30
red ripe tomatoes, 39
ricotta, 40
ricotta cheese, 16, 24, 32, 38, 45, 52
roasted pumpkin flesh*, 33
roasted red peppers, 6
romano cheese, 1, 18
rosemary, 22
rosemary sprigs, 43
russet potatoes, 9
salad oil, 18, 18, 36
salt, 1, 3, 6, 8, 11, 12, 13, 16, 16, 19, 27, 28, 28, 30, 32, 32, 36, 40, 41, 42, 43, 45, 45, 46, 46, 49, 51, 52, 54, 57, 61
salt and pepper, 4, 4, 7, 24, 24, 52
salt and pepper to taste, 18, 33, 44, 56
sauce, 11
sausage, 41
scallions, 28, 53, 53, 60
see * note, 57, 62
seeded and chopped, 12
seeded and cut into, 1
seeded chopped unpeeled tomato, 50
sesame oil, 30
setting to 4 sheet, 57
shallots, 2, 12, 39, 60
sheets filo, 13
shortening, 8, 27
shortening or oil, 50
shredded carrot, 11
shredded mozzarella cheese,, 38

shrimp, 38
sifted flour, 7, 45
small butternut squash, 15
small chicken stock, 22
small chinese, 29
small onion, 11
soft bread crumbs, 18
softened, 27
sour cream, 9
soy sauce, 30
spaghetti sauce, 15, 37, 50
spaghetti sauce with mushroom, 19
spicy vegetable vinaigrette, 50
spicy vegetable vinaigrette:, 50
spinach, 18, 19
spinach; frozen, 18
spinach;small, 34
sprig rosemary, 4
sprigs fresh rosemary leaves, 6
sprigs fresh thyme leaves, 6
sprigs rosemary, 46
stalk celery, 4
steamed, 24
stewed tomatoes with peppers, 6
sugar, 8, 13, 27, 30, 59
sweet butter, 57
swiss chard, 40
teapoon salt, 7
thawed if frozen, 33
thin, 1
thin asparagus spears, 42
thinly sliced, 21
to taste, 28, 40, 57
toasted pine nuts, 33
tomato paste, 18, 32
tomato sauce, 6, 18, 19, 60
tomato sauce) or meat sauce, 34
tomatoes, 60
tomatoes*, 41
tomatoes; italian plum, 12
torn escarole, 43
turkey cutlets, 55
unbleached flour, 32

Index

unbleached white flour, 1
unsalted butter, 9, 24, 28
up to 1 cup, 49
vanilla, 8, 27, 59
veal glaze, 20
vegetable oil, 23, 30, 54
vegetable oil for frying, 15
vegetable or chicken stock, 41, 56
very cold water, 45
virgin olive oil, 57
walnuts, 8, 13
walnuts pcs, 3
warm spinach salad with pancetta, 46
warm water, 7
warmed, 37
water, 12, 13, 15, 16, 22, 22, 29, 30, 36, 49, 51, 56, 62

water chestnuts, 30
whipping cream, 12
whipping cream - well chilled, 59
white chocolate bars,, 58
white flour, 38
white truffle oil**, 9
white truffle paste,, 9
white wine, 2, 11, 12, 56
whole egg, 56
won ton skins, 47
won ton wrappers,, 33
won-ton wrappers, 20, 43
wonton wrappers, 9, 50
wonton wrappers -, 62
yellow pepper, 56
zucchini, 38, 56

Made in the USA
Lexington, KY
08 October 2015